EXPLORATIONS IN
INDEXING AND ABSTRACTING

LIBRARY AND INFORMATION
SCIENCE TEXT SERIES

EXPLORATIONS IN INDEXING AND ABSTRACTING

POINTING, VIRTUE, AND POWER

Brian C. O'Connor

1996
Libraries Unlimited, Inc.
Englewood, Colorado

LIBRARIES UNLIMITED, INC.
P.O. Box 6633
Englewood, CO 80155-6633
(800) 237-6124

Production Editor: Stephen Haenel
Copy Editor: Brooke Graves
Proofreader: Ann Marie Damian
Editorial Assistant: Shannon Graff
Typesetting and Interior Design: Michael Florman

Library of Congress Cataloging-in-Publication Data

O'Connor, Brian C., 1947-
    Explorations in indexing and abstracting : pointing, virtue, and
power / Brian C. O'Connor.
    xiii, 182 p. 17x25 cm. -- (Library and information science text series)
    Includes bibliographical references and index.
    ISBN 1-56308-184-9
    1. Indexing. 2. Abstracting. I. Title. II. Series.
Z695.9.026 1996
025.3--dc20   96-18333
                                                      CIP

*Dedicated with affection
and appreciation to
Ethan and Andrew*

Contents

Preface

There are too many books, too many records, too many photographs, too many newspapers, too many journals, too many CD-ROMs, too many World Wide Web sites. No one person can read all the printed works, even those printed just in one language. Millions of people around the world are connected to the Internet and traffic on the Net is increasing rapidly. No one person can listen to all the recorded music or watch all the video productions or become familiar with all the sites on the Net. One must choose which very tiny portion of all the documents available one will use for education, entertainment, or decision making.

We live in the midst of phenomenal changes in production, dissemination, and use of information. The numbers of information sources are growing at a staggering rate. In 1777, the Dartmouth College Library opened with 305 books. It would take until 1970 to reach 1 million books, but only another two decades to reach 2 million books. The collection that Thomas Jefferson sold to Congress after the destruction of the Capitol in the War of 1812 consisted of about 6,000 books. The collection now numbers in the many millions. The number of people with connections to the Internet is about the same as the population of the entire United States in the middle of the nineteenth century.

The very nature of information sources is changing. For the cost of one hardcover book, one can purchase a CD-ROM that contains the texts of nearly 2,000 literary works, along with spoken-word selections, music, and a search engine that can find all uses of a word in only a few seconds. Children in over 50 countries routinely chat about war, earthquakes, dating, popular music, and television shows on the KidCafe network. Photographs and movies can now be stored in desktop computers. Telephone numbers for most of the country and street maps for the entire United States are available for home computers on CD-ROMs. Some scholarly journals are appearing only in electronic form, giving rise to questions about the very nature of scholarly publication.

We might well ask just what sort of role indexing and abstracting could play in such a world. What are the challenges and the opportunities? What could indexing and abstracting be like in an environment with machinery that can search texts at speeds far greater than humanly possible? What are optimal designs for indexing and abstracting in a multimedia environment? What new questions can we ask now that the nature of documents is changing?

The subtitle of this book, *Pointing, Virtue, and Power*, summarizes the concepts underlying the responses to such questions. Thus, they are at the heart of this book. *Pointing* is the fundamental definition of *indexing;* that is, an index is some form of pointing device, directing a user to useful material. *Virtue,* when used in speaking of a thing, means the efficacy, worth, or power of that thing; the distillation of that efficacy lies at the heart of the definition of *abstract*. Together, indexing and abstracting are the primary tools that provide a person with *power* to make meaningful use of the information contained in the myriad of recorded documents available. Explorations is used in this book's title in the sense of "finding out the condition of" something or "ranging over for the purpose of discovery."

Several elements are crucial to this text:

- The searcher or patron is central to any retrieval system
- A subject is not an inherent element of a text
- Patron-specific concepts should be made available to the patron
- The tagging of concepts should be meaningful to the patron
- Computers open possibilities for customizing access to documents

> Behind the use of the definite article, the subject, lies an apparently innocent assumption that there will be just one thing to mention in answer to the question "What is it about?" . . . [W]hat seems to us to stand out depends on us as well as on the writing.[1]

There are, of course, already schemes for describing and organizing documents. Yet these can be useless or even counterproductive if they are not applied with a considerable understanding of what will be truly useful for any individual searcher. Some people come to systems with clear concepts of what sort of material would satisfy their requirements; some come with vague concepts, but would likely recognize something useful if it were presented; some come with no preconceived ideas but only a desire to shake up what they know in hopes of a new discovery.

For each person, finding something that relates to the question means finding a useful piece of information. It generally matters little whether it comes as a whole book, a paragraph, an illustration, a collection of books and videos, or conversations with an expert.

Failure to present an aspect of a document that might have been useful (or indicated utility), or failure to represent a useful aspect in a manner appropriate to the searcher, means that a potential answer will go unfound. This suggests the need for dynamic systems that incorporate the user in some fashion. Even in established systems, consideration of user characteristics may enhance system performance.

Approach of This Text

Grappling with the question *What is it about?*, in order to design systems to foster successful searching, is at the heart of this book. Its stimulus is the thesis that no matter how facile the retrieval system, substantial failures result because of fundamental differences between the manner in which documents have been represented and the manner in which searchers represent their questions.

The relationship between a person with a question and a source of information is complex. Indexing and abstracting often fail because too much emphasis has been put on the mechanics of description and too little has been given to what ought to be represented. Research literature suggests that inappropriate representation results in failed searches a significant number of times, perhaps even in a majority of cases.

For these reasons, this text emphasizes modeling and constructing appropriate representations of each question and each document. Such an approach mirrors the thoughts of wildlife photographer Paul Rezendes on searching:

Many people today think tracking is simply finding a trail and following it to the animal that made it. . . . I think the true meaning of reading tracks and signs in the forest has been pushed into the background by an overemphasis on finding the next track. . . . If you spend half an hour finding the next track, you may have learned a lot about finding the next track but not much about the animal. If you spend time learning about the animal and its ways, you may be able to find the next track without looking. . . . Tracking an animal . . . brings you closer to it in perception.[2]

Students in programs of information studies will find focal points for discussion about system design and refinement of existing systems. Working scholars and others who work within large document collections, whether paper or electronic, will find insights into the strengths and weaknesses of access systems. They may also find validation of their personal methods of searching.

Many access systems are less than self-evident in their design. It is not at all unusual to find tenured faculty members who do not know that there is actually a system behind the Library of Congress Subject Headings used on documents in their university library. Users of large on-line databases often do not understand that they may have to use a list of sanctioned terms rather than words off the tops of their heads. They often do not realize the consequences of different forms of request constructions.

In these pages, we consider means by which we might represent both documents and questions so as to enable successful searching. The first chapters set a foundation of models and concepts of representation, document characteristics, and question characteristics. The following exercises and case studies are intended to foster close consideration of the elements of a successful search in a variety of settings.

Again, this text is not intended to be a manual of indexing and abstracting practice. It is not intended to replace the numerous exemplary manuals now available; we give only passing consideration to many of the standards, current practices, and systems that are so well covered in other texts. A final section addresses some generalities that emerge from the previous chapters. It also reviews where we have been and where we might yet go.

Notes

1. Patrick Wilson, *Two Kinds of Power: An Essay on Bibliographic Control* (Berkeley: University of California Press, 1968).

2. Paul Rezendes, *Tracking and the Art of Seeing: How to Read Animal Tracks and Signs* (Charlotte, Vt.: Camden House, 1992).

Acknowledgments

Humbling is perhaps the most appropriate description for the experience of constructing an introductory text. "You've gotta teach to learn," a line from a blues song, reminds one of what a privilege it is to have engaged and enthusiastic students. My sincere thanks are offered to the students in my courses on indexing, abstracting, and representation.

The mentors and researchers whose efforts are the foundation for my work deserve both great appreciation and apologies. To Theodora Hodges, Patrick Wilson, M. E. Maron, William Cooper, and Bertrand Augst, I say thanks for demonstrating the necessity of a concern with fundamental problems and for firing passion for the multifaceted entity of human representation and discourse. To the many researchers in mathematics, management, philosophy, computer science, and art upon whom I have drawn quite liberally, I say thank you. To my mentors and the researchers both known and unmet, I offer apologies for drawing bits and pieces and cobbling them together in sometimes rather rough ways. I can only hope that the final product will speak well to your influences. I am honored to stand on your shoulders, if hesitantly, and gladly acknowledge that any mistakes or misrepresentations are my own.

Many people take part in the construction of a text. Author statements should probably include "prompted, goaded, spell-checked, critiqued, and suffered by. . . ." The fine people at Libraries Unlimited were most gracious in their accommodation of my idiosyncrasies and extraordinarily capable in their tasks. I give my special thanks to Kim Dority for thoughtful comments on the text and gracious response to my moments of crisis; to Steve Haenel for his shepherding of the project, especially the technical aspects; to Brooke Graves for her thorough and enlightening copyediting; and to David Loertscher, formerly of Libraries Unlimited, for his belief in the project.

My very special thanks to my colleagues at the School of Library and Information Management at Emporia State University, to Ed Pai for critical comments, and to Mary Keeney O'Connor for conceptual advice, tolerance, and loving encouragement.

Chapter 1
Background Concepts

Basic Models

We know that if information is required, the first move is usually to consult nearby sources: a neighbor, a friend with some expertise, or a book in the home. If these are not satisfactory in resolving the need, then a collection of recorded information is a possible solution. We must remember, though, that it is a solution with a price. Even under the best circumstances of searching, there is an investment in time and, probably, an investment of intellectual energy to analyze and synthesize the new material.

In its simplest form, as in figure 1.1, the model of a user approaching a document collection in hopes of filling an information gap has only two elements: a person with some requirement for information and a collection of documents. Unless the collection is very small and very specialized, so that every work happens to be a good response, the user will have to make some selection from among the documents. A representation or sample of the collection is required. That is, some works are chosen or extracted, whereas others are left behind. Even in the unlikely event of a collection in which every document is a good response, available time may compel the user to take a smaller subset of the documents.

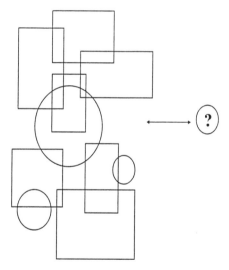

Fig. 1.1. The general problem: Searcher and document collection.

1

This selection could be made by going through all the documents and selecting those that meet the appropriate criteria, as in figure 1.2. This assumes that the searcher knows what those criteria are, that good responses can be recognized, and that time and other resources are available to conduct such a search.

A solution to the dilemma of making a selection within a reasonable amount of time is to make representations of the documents. Indexing and abstracting are systems of representation. Typically, representations of the whole collection are made, stating: "the materials on a particular topic are to be found here; those on another topic, over there." Indexing by subject headings points to clusters of works. At the same time, representations are made of each work, so that a searcher need read or view or listen to only a small document. Abstracting reduces each work to its essence, making a secondary document to stand in place of the original. Then, individual documents often have their own indexes (back-of-book index, table of contents) to point the way to regions containing particular concepts.

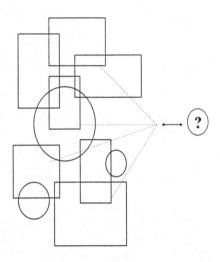

Fig. 1.2. Locating relevant works and sifting useful material from the mass.

We have said nothing yet about the mechanisms of making the representations, or what the rules are, or who constructs the rules. At this point we are looking only at the general model, as modeled in figure 1.3 on page 3, in which representations of documents and representations of questions are compared in some manner. The results of that comparison will be a set of documents (or citations to documents).

Patrons cannot yet simply put their heads down on a reference desk, or a keyboard, or a card catalog and have the system know the nature of their information needs. The technology is not yet in place and our understanding of the nature of question states is still crude. Thus, issues of representation of questions and documents are central to indexing and abstracting.

Linked closely to issues of representation are issues of the system used to compare questions with documents. The mechanisms for making use of representations to put the most appropriate set of documents at the patron's disposal must also be central to our explorations of indexing and abstracting.

Information loss is one of the most important elements of the general model. *Representation,* by definition, means that some information will be left behind or left out, as suggested in figure 1.3. Ensuring that the necessary loss of information is not fatal to the search effort is one of the crucial tasks of indexing and abstracting. Our job is to decide which information is expendable.

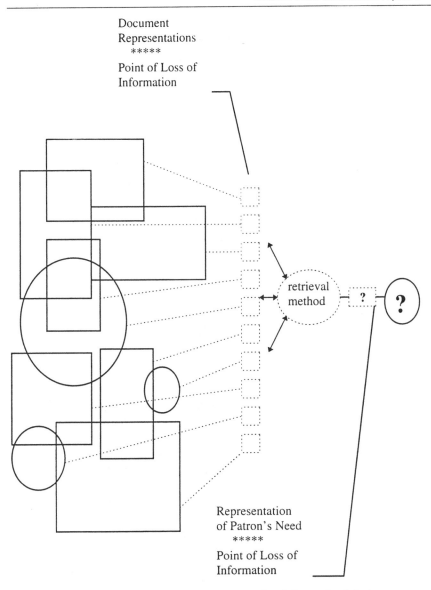

Document
Representations
*****
Point of Loss of
Information

retrieval
method

?

?

Representation
of Patron's Need
*****
Point of Loss of
Information

Fig. 1.3. Tradeoff of representation: Time is saved, but information is lost.

Search Time and Search Space

We can call the set of all the available documents the *search space* and we can call the time a user spends in the search space the *search time*. We can say that at one end of a spectrum of search time and space is the instance of having to do no searching at all. A person who has no requirement for outside information sources need not spend any time nor look at any documents. Similarly, a person who has been given a title or the location of a work may have to spend a little bit of time actually getting the work, but will not have to spend any time searching for which work to get.

Search time that is too great is the flaw in the search method at the other end of the spectrum. In some ways, it would be very reasonable to say to the person coming into a document collection with an information requirement: "start at document one; go all the way through it; move to document two; go all the way through it; continue this process until you find what you need." Unfortunately, this makes some assumptions that are not always correct.

The least worrisome assumption is that the person would actually recognize the document or documents that would be right. Would the person have the critical and conceptual abilities necessary to recognize such documents? Would a more elementary work have to be encountered first in order for the appropriate document to be sensible? Would the passage of time during the search affect what would be the best response or even the validity of the question?

Time is the more vexing assumption. Even if we were to reduce the number of documents from all those available in one language to just those available in a modest academic library, time would remain a problem. If we assume 500,000 documents in a modest academic collection, and if we grant that a person could read or view or listen to 10 each day, 135 years would pass before all the documents had been seen. Clearly this is not suitable.

Of course, it might be that good materials would be found well before the end of the collection had been reached. Yet the numbers remain instructive. For most users of document collections, there must be means for trimming down the search time and the search space. There must be means for looking at only some portion of the collection. There must also be means for examining that small portion more quickly than by reading each and every document in its entirety.

Indexing reduces search space. Abstracting reduces evaluation time. Together, indexing and abstracting reduce search time. Sophisticated and appropriate means of reducing search time and search space are required if people are to make full use of accumulated recorded knowledge.

Context

We must now establish a context for our considerations of indexing and abstracting as the means of reducing search space and search time. First we will sketch the intellectual discipline within which these modes of representation are studied; then it will be useful to establish some touchstone definitions for foundational terms. The physical environment within which documents are sought will be established as a significant element, and models of primary issues and relationships will be proposed. A metaphor will set the stage for our investigations.

Theory of the organization of information is the common term for the discipline within which we find the study of indexing and abstracting. Looking into the catalog of a doctoral program for an outline of the field, we might find something such as:

Fundamental Concepts

- information
- aboutness
- relevance
- closeness of meaning

Basic Design Concepts

- document identification
- indexing
- abstracting
- classification
- search languages
- query formulation

Automated Systems Techniques

- associative search techniques
- clustering
- automatic extraction
- full text retrieval
- genetic algorithms

Evaluation

- system performance
- user satisfaction

Advanced Design Principles

- vector space model
- probabilistic indexing
- utility theoretic indexing
- community memory construction
- inductive searches

Knowledge Representation

- formal logic
- relational calculi
- artificial intelligence
- neurophysiological insights

Such an outline situates the concepts of indexing and abstracting within a robust theoretical framework.[1] This provides us with avenues of exploration, evaluation, and speculation. The outline summarizes questions such as:

- Just what do we mean by *information?*
- How does someone know what a document is "about"?
- Is the same work "about" the same thing to different persons?
- What makes a document significant or *relevant* for someone?
- Just what do we mean by indexing and abstracting?
- How do we do indexing and abstracting?
- How do we make a question?
- What do we have to tell a computer to have it index or abstract?
- What do we have to know about documents and questions?
- What does *efficiency* mean?

- What is good indexing or good abstracting?
- How do people get all those things into their minds?
- How can we embody questions and concepts for manipulation?

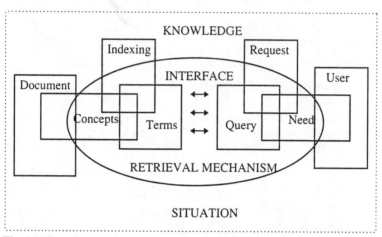

Fig. 1.4. Complex web of relations between a user and a document.

These are the sorts of questions that are raised and elaborated upon in the following chapters. Case studies and discussions, together with bibliographic essays, frame possible responses, or at least paths for exploration. The complex web of relations that mark the territory is sketched in figure 1.4. This map is an elaboration of the models in figures 1.1, 1.2, and 1.3. It hints at the numerous subtle yet crucial distinctions that must be made when discussing documents and their users.[2] For example, both the author of a work and a user exist within a knowledge framework and within some situation that compels the authoring of a work or the seeking of a work. The degree of similarity between the settings will likely determine, to some degree, the utility of a particular document to a particular user.

Similarly, a user may have a need for information, but be capable of expressing it only partially; thus, there may be a difference between the need and the request. Also, the request may not be in terms useful to the search system, so there might have to be a translation from the user's request to the actual query put to the system.

Definitions of Terms

Consensus is lacking on concise definitions for many of the terms fundamental to discussions of indexing and abstracting. Differing camps within disciplines ranging from philosophy to artificial intelligence are still puzzling and arguing over the mechanisms of knowing, understanding, and reasoning. Therefore, it is not possible to give simple, unambiguous, widely accepted explanations of:

data	abstracting
information	classification
knowledge	reasoning
wisdom	representation
indexing	organization

However, it is necessary that we have some common vocabulary for our subsequent explorations. Therefore, working definitions of the preceding terms are presented here, then refined, adjusted, and elaborated upon as we consider specific problems and issues.

Data, information, knowledge, and wisdom are generally taken to be related in some sort of hierarchical way, each one being more refined, advanced, or rare. Even within any one set of definitions, the boundaries are not solid and well established.

Data is generally taken as the beginning of the progression. The word is actually the plural form of a Latin word meaning "something that is given." Dictionary definitions tend to be of this sort:

> Fact[s], proposition[s], etc., granted or known, from which other facts are to be deduced.

> Something given or admitted, esp. as a basis for reasoning or inference

Yet note the confusion that arises in the *Oxford American Dictionary:*

> Facts or *information* [emphasis added] to be used as a basis for discussing or deciding something. . . .

For our purposes, *data* will be considered input that has not yet been evaluated or given a context. There is a comedy routine that gives us a good example:

> News broadcaster: "And now for some football scores. 23, 17, 6, 42, and 12."

Without a context, these are just numbers. We may recognize them as being within the ordinary range of scores in a football game, but we can gain little more from this string of data. We do not know if any of these are to be taken in pairs, if they are just the winning scores from each of five games, if they are scores from today's games, or if they even have any relation to any real games at all. The numbers are simply data.

Similarly, a thermometer reading of 37 degrees is data that can be made useful or meaningful only if given a context. Is it that temperature here? Now? On which scale of measurement? Am I going outside? Is this a lot colder or warmer than it has been lately?

Information is probably the term on our list with the most diffuse set of definitions. The word comes from two Latin words, "in" and "forma," which suggest the form or shape inside. Definitions in the literature range from statistical measures of the degree of uncertainty in a system; to "anything I can forget"; to changes in the mental maps by which we operate in the world;[3] to Wheeler's "the quantum presents us with physics as information."[4]

Ordinary dictionary definitions do little to resolve the issue. "[I]ntelligence gathered or communicated" simply adds another term for which there is no simple definition. "[C]ommunication or reception of knowledge or intelligence" adds two more terms, one of which (*knowledge*) jumps ahead in our taxonomy. It also implies that communication is a one-way event—an assumption that we will soon abandon. "Facts told, heard, or discovered" adds the term *facts*, yet another word for our list.

What we can see in the terms *intelligence, knowledge,* and *facts* is an acknowledgment that "information" has a connotation of evaluation, context, and consensus. Data have been reduced, modeled, and tested within some accepted framework. We suggest that *information is the reduction and synthesis of data for use in reasoning.*[5]

Both *knowledge* and *wisdom* remain beyond easy definition. Each implies a greater degree of reduction, synthesis, and analysis of data, together with community agreement about the means of reduction and the value of the resulting outputs. In our present taxonomy, we might find it useful to make a distinction between *information* and *knowledge* based on concepts from evolutionary epistemology.

Plotkin suggests that knowledge is what gives our lives order and that "knowing is living and surviving."[6] We might say that *information* is an acceptable internal picture of the world, whereas *knowledge* is the successful use of internal pictures. Generally we think of these as occurring locally, within an individual, yet they could also be taken to happen to groups over years or generations. Both ideas and physical adaptations are generated, tested, and regenerated. We could say that knowledge is the set of ideas and adaptations that is working at the time. This suggests the possibility that knowledge may change—may have to change—as environments change.

It is important to note that wisdom need not be seen as universal. The counsel that seems wise in one group of people may seem utterly ridiculous to another group that holds a different paradigm. Rock-and-roll music was the expressive force and metaphor for some lives, yet was ignored, vilified, and condemned by others. To those who held to an earth-centered view of the universe, Galileo and Copernicus were raving lunatics, yet they are now heroes in our textbooks. To some, Darwinian explanations of the workings of the world are of little value, yet to others they are powerful explanatory tools.

While it will be necessary for us to consider what any individual user of an information system considers knowledge, there is probably no need to posit a formal definition beyond the concept of both knowledge and wisdom being, to varying degrees, evaluated and accepted information.

Indexing is considered here in just brief and general terms, because it is a primary topic of our explorations and will be refined and expanded as we encounter a variety of situations requiring some form of indexing. The term *index* is derived from a Greek word meaning "to point." Whether we are speaking of a back-of-the-book index, a classification scheme, or a subject index to a whole collection of works, the elements of the index serve as signs pointing to some smaller subset of a whole.

We must be careful not to be unduly influenced by any particular concepts of the term that we hold from tradition and practice. The general idea of signs pointing toward a subset of information may well manifest itself in very different ways, especially in the newly developing digital environment.

Abstracting comes from Latin words meaning "drag out"; indeed, we get the word *tractor* from the same root. Samuel Johnson in an example used by the *Oxford English Dictionary,* offers a powerful and poetic definition: "a smaller quantity containing the virtue and power of a greater." The operative definitions within the practice of abstracting stem from the American National Standards Institute. ANSI speaks to the "smaller quantity" by suggesting a numerical value (generally one-tenth to one-twentieth the length of the original) and to the means of achieving that size. The nature of "virtue and power" are not addressed so expressly.

In a sense, *virtue* and *power* suggest that we are speaking of the heart of the matter, of the most fundamental aspect of something. This runs counter to the daily use of the term *abstract,* which suggests an ethereal nature that is hard to grasp. If one thinks of the military context within which the term *abstract* was once used, another issue arises. *Abstract* was apparently used by Roman armies as a term for pillaging conquered cities. To some, the virtue and power resided in the beautiful women; to others, in the strong men; to others, in the jewels and other riches; to yet others, in the religious objects. The saying "one person's trash is another's treasure" is apt here. To abstract is to pull out the virtue and power of some larger entity or set of entities, but these could well be different for different people.

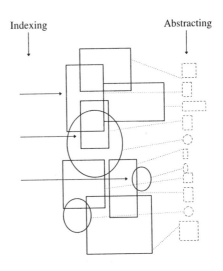

Fig. 1.5. Indexing and abstracting: Pointing and "dragging out" the essence.

As with indexing, we must be careful not to be constrained by our current notions of abstracting. Can we design systems that can detect the treasure for each user? Can we abstract multimedia documents? Must abstracts be constructed a priori, or might we design systems for ad hoc construction of custom-designed abstracts?

Figure 1.5 shows the general relationship between indexing, abstracting, and a document collection. Indexing points to areas of likely utility, while abstracting provides smaller, secondary documents for inspection. Indexing and abstracting of some sort are absolute necessities for navigating through the sea of information in which we find ourselves today. However, they must be accomplished in ways hospitable to and compatible with those who make use of them.

Classification is another concept closely tied to the reduction of search time. The Latin term "classis" meant a group called to military service or, more generally, a social group. This became extended to the idea of any group of things sharing some common attribute or set of attributes. Generally, there will be fewer groups of things than there will be individual entities; thus, less examination is required to find a desired entity. What we must remember is that there are many instances in which a single entity can hold membership within several groups and that there are groups with less-than-strict membership rules. We may think of classification as putting like with like, but we must remember to ask what we mean by *like.*[7]

Putting things in groups helps us to act rapidly. It can be argued that classification is a survival skill. If we had to compute the threat quotient or the food quotient of every single animal we encountered in the wild, we would not survive for long. Knowing that most instances of "large plus sharp teeth plus claws" mean fight or flight is more efficient than having to assess the consequences of size and the potential of sharp teeth and claws acting on the human body in each instance.

Of course, such classification can easily become what we disparagingly call stereotyping. The inappropriate attribution of characteristics and the subsequent inappropriate actions can cause difficulties. Similar difficulties can arise whether we are talking about encountering animals, dealing with people, or organizing documents.

Reasoning is closely linked with all the concepts discussed so far. It is the subject of probably one of the longest-running debates in history, dating at least to the time of the major Greek philosophers and probably before. Although this is not the arena for sorting out the various approaches to the nature of thought, we can say that information and the ways it is structured and utilized are fundamental to reasoning. Most of the efforts of the field of organization of information are focused on enhancing reasoning ability.

We take reasoning in a very broad sense here, to include both the logico-sequential abilities we sometimes label left-brained, as well as the spatial and holistic abilities of right-brained thinking. Reason is considered to be the faculties we use to:

- plan for the future by examining our past and present

- weigh differing possible actions

- make our way about in daily life based on all the data pouring in

- play with ideas and reshape them

At this point we would do well to consider very briefly the characteristics of three primary sorts of reasoning. We do this because there is a close relationship between these sorts of reasoning and the changes in representation that the digital information environment may allow.

Deductive reasoning is the sort probably most often associated with "logical" thinking. It consists of rules for deriving true statements from preexisting true statements. One of the most common illustrations of this sort of reasoning is this construction about the Greek philosopher Socrates:

All men are mortal. [a true statement]

Socrates is a man. [a true statement with a link to the previous one]

Therefore, Socrates is mortal.

Deductive reasoning seems to be at the heart of much of information retrieval apparatus developed over the past century. Whether because of philosophical compulsion or economic necessity, most systems have had:

- strictly defined and unitary placement of documents within a classification

- questions restricted to topic descriptions

- deductive links between a question, collection documents, and documents put into a user's hands

Of course, many things in life do not easily fit into such small packets of truth. Also, we often have to make decisions without complete data, so the issue of stringing all necessary truth statements into logical chains, as in deductive reasoning, is meaningless. Similarly, questions in an information system may not always be easily articulable in precise terms.

Inductive reasoning is one method we use to cope with incomplete data and lack of time. Here we use the constraints that suggest a possible answer or set of answers and rule out some possible answers. A simple example can be used to demonstrate this sort of reasoning:

2, 4, 6, 8, _____

If we now say "Fill in the blank," there are many possible answers but only a few that are likely. These could be the digits of street addresses, so that 2,4,6,9 would follow in the blank space. These could be digits in a repeating set—2,4,6,8,2,4,6,8,2,4,6,8. . . . These could be the first few digits in a randomly selected group that just happened to fall into a sequence of incrementing by two—2, 4, 6, 8, 37, 92, 103, 54, 13, 27. The more likely responses, because of various combinations of what we are taught about numbers and what we are socially conditioned to do with numbers, are

2, 4, 6, 8, 10, 12, 14, 16, etc., adding two to each previous number

or

"Who do we appreciate?!," using rhyme and meter for a chant

Analogical reasoning seems to suit humans well. It could be said to be at the foundation of education, classification, and metaphor. Every time we think to ourselves or say to another: "It's like a . . . " or "It works just like a . . . " or "It's kind of like . . . ," we are using analogical reasoning. We use what we know about one system or thing to understand or explain something that is not well known.

A popular song had a phrase "My baby, he's like a freight train." Given the rest of the lyrics, it was clear that the woman was not singing about a child less than a year old. She was singing about her affection for an age-appropriate man. We use the term *baby* because the physiological responses and the accompanying feelings of devotion and tenderness most people feel for babies are similar to the feelings in a romantic relationship. The term *baby* makes clear the sort of feelings and their depth.

Clearly, the man is not made of steel, does not run on diesel fuel, does not weigh hundreds of tons, and does not spend his life on railroad tracks. He is not a freight train. However, he does have a habit of coming into town, staying only briefly, then leaving again. The emotional impact on the woman singing the song is one of devastation—as if she had been run over by a freight train. She has not been crushed, she is not bleeding and dying—she has not actually been run over by a train. She does feel incapable of conducting a normal life; chemical levels in the body have changed to induce some pain and inability to move; thoughts are too distracted to pursue daily affairs. The feelings and consequences of the man leaving town, as a freight train does, are such that she might as well have been run over by the train.

Representation is the set of means by which one thing stands for another. The *Oxford English Dictionary* speaks of "the fact of expressing or denoting by means of a figure or symbol," as well as "to bring clearly and distinctly before the mind . . . by description." Representation is a complex web of attributes of disparate objects and concepts, idiosyncratic and socially constructed codes and agreements, and neurological abilities. Paraphrasing Marr, we can say that representation is a system for extracting or highlighting some characteristics of concepts or things, along with an explanation of the rules and reasons for that extraction.[8]

A representation is not just another instance of the original. It presents only some characteristics of the original. Generally, it is shorter, smaller, or less time-consuming than the original. For some purposes, it stands in place of the original.

Two important points are implied by this definition. If someone does not know the rules and procedures for the representation, it may be of little or no use. We need only to look to the studies on catalog use or our own observations of card catalogs and on-line catalogs to see the importance of this aspect of the definition. The majority of users do not seem to understand that:

- There is a sanctioned list of subject headings
- Subject headings are complex constructs
- Subject headings represent the whole document
- Odds are very low for guessing the subject heading on a work

That is, they do not know the procedures for representing documents that we call Library of Congress Subject Headings, or Dewey Classification, or post-coordinate Boolean searches.

Also, if some things are highlighted, by definition some things are left behind. In an information environment, the decision of what to leave behind can be vexing. How can we know which parts of a book can be ignored or generalized into a broad subject heading? Can we really represent audio and video works just with words? Are patrons really concerned that the information in a library happens to come in segments of 200 or 300 pages at a time? Can we really leave out levels of detail smaller than the book? Could we leave out a large percentage of the collection entirely and concentrate in detail on a small, representative set of documents?

Organization is where theory and practice meld. The word comes from a Greek term meaning "work." Organization puts to work all the elements we have discussed, as they relate to people seeking information. It enables those people to work productively.

If we look to the *Oxford English Dictionary* definition of *organization,* we get the sense of putting organs together into a vital system. It may be appropriate to keep this biological metaphor. We seek to have systems that respond to differing needs and differing circumstances. The complexity of creatures with numerous organs suits them to survival in changing environments. Organization does not simply mean arranging things in some way. Rather, it implies that elements are put into play to facilitate some activity. *System* is the term we will use for the results of organizing—that is, "a set of connected . . . parts . . . that work together."

Technological Environment

The environment for our explorations of indexing and abstracting is at once compelling and awesome; weighted with the baggage of tradition, yet informed by generations of consideration and practice; the beneficiary of technologies almost beyond belief only a few years ago, yet the potential victim of technology lifted above reason and compassion.

We are on the threshold of redefining what library and information services can be.[9] We are in the midst of a significant change, a point of major discontinuity with the practices and potential of previous models of information systems. The significance of this threshold is made clear by an adaptation of Buckland's model of the evolution of library service:

- **Paper**—technical processes, catalog, and documents all paper

- **Automated**—technical processes and catalog on computer, but documents are still the same paper documents

- **Electronic**—technical processes, catalog, and documents are all digital

For the library, the paper model meant a considerable amount of warehousing work just to keep the system functioning. Large numbers of pieces of paper were generated and handled for ordering and then cataloging each book. Each book had to be shelved and reshelved after use.

For the patron, the paper model meant going to the library (if it was open), going to the catalog, and then going somewhere else to find the document. If the document was already in use, the patron was out of luck. If the patron wanted to incorporate parts of documents into a paper or book, hand-copying or photocopying were the primary alternatives—rarely did libraries allow cutting up of library book pages for inclusion in a patron's work!

The automated phase, in which many systems now find themselves, has reduced the amount of paperwork for the libraries. Perhaps more importantly, it has meant that the patron no longer has to physically travel to the library to check on its contents. The patron no neet not wait until the physical building is open to do catalog work. Access from home or office to libraries around the world is now commonplace. The documents are still available only to one patron at a time during business hours and they still cannot be cut and pasted. Still, a shift toward making the patron's work more efficient has taken place.

The electronic library is fundamentally different. Documents in the form of digital files can be accessed in the same way as the automated catalog—from outside the library building, at hours beyond those of the physical library. This means that documents can be available whenever the patron requires them. A large number of patrons can have access to the same document at the same time. The digitizing of text, sound, and images means not only that cut-and-paste is possible, but also that it can be done in a multimedia environment.

Such an environment raises numerous issues. Can we design dynamic and linked combinations of a text, its abstract, and any bibliographies in which it might be listed? What will be the fiscal and political boundaries for acquiring, storing, and using files? Where do issues of copyright, fair use, and intellectual property reside in the digital environment? Will the public library become the housing for hundreds of terminals and only a few books for novelty?

The intellectual environment is changing as well. More and more research is centering on the user's role in retrieval systems. Definitions of relevance are coming to include user attributes. The mathematics and database design concepts behind complex retrieval systems are finding support in desktop computers with sufficient computing capability to realize them outside the laboratory.

Much of common practice from the paper era, and to a large extent from the automated era as well, stems from system limitations. Although there is theory-level discussion behind the practice of giving subject headings at the level of the whole book, one need not look far to see that the practice is a result of the limitations of the paper system. The hours required to generate subject terms at a more specific level would be prohibitive. Also, the number of pieces of paper that required typing and filing would be beyond the fiscal and temporal capabilities of any agency.

The challenge of the electronic era will be to use the system capabilities for rapid execution of mundane tasks to its greatest extent. Doing what is done now, only faster, would likely be of benefit. However, it is in the promise of machine capability that efficient, workable, user-centered systems lie.

Trains Have No Steering Wheels: A Metaphor ————

Railroad locomotives are not equipped with steering wheels. In a very real sense, the steering has been accomplished beforehand. Those who placed the rails accomplished all the steering. This contributes to the efficiency of moving freight and passengers around the country. Huge loads of items large and small can be moved by train to different parts of the country in days. Anyone can board a train and relax while being transported over large distances.

So long as the passenger has in mind a destination and that destination is on or near the rail line, this is a good system. However, rapid and easy movement along established lines and to established points may not necessarily be efficient. The passenger whose destination is not on the line may travel the rails as a part of the journey, yet take a bus or car some considerable distance as another part. The traveler seeking the "feel" of an area may wish to travel on foot or bicycle to take in the minutiae. The geologist or archaeologist may have to leave all roads entirely. The salesperson or politician may have to stop in places and at times that cannot be accommodated by rail lines, and so must take a bus or an airplane.

Efficiency is a measure of the degree to which certain goals or criteria are met. The speed of operation of a system, its fuel economy, its percentage of downtime, and its load capacity may be efficiency measures for some people, but not for others. Each user of a train is faced with questions, such as: Does it go where I want to go? Does it do so in a suitable time frame? Is the cost appropriate to the gain? The rail lines are highly efficient for some purposes, moderately so for some, and not at all for others.

Indexing and abstracting are similar to train systems. In most instances, the steering has been accomplished beforehand. Indexing terms have been constructed or extracted, classification categories established, and abstracts written before a system user engages the system. So long as the user has a good grasp of what is being sought and can put a question into system terms, most systems are efficient. Yet, for the patron not familiar with system vocabulary, for the patron with a functional requirement that cannot easily be put into topical terms, and for the scholar seeking new connections, most systems are only moderately efficient at best.

Designing indexing and abstracting systems to be efficient requires an understanding of the goals to be served by the system. In most instances this will mean knowing the sorts of results any individual user will desire from the system. Some users may be pleased with results achieved within the current mode of dividing and describing the world of knowledge. Other users may require systems of very different sorts.

The traveler in a landscape of documents requires the same elements as a traveler in the geographic landscape. Both require means of navigating, moving about, and evaluating progress.

Bibliographic Environment

Considerations of how we might enable access to material to be found in a large collection of documents are informed by a wide range of fields of study. It is unlikely that even several pages of bibliographic citations could adequately encompass the numerous authors, schools, paradigmatic discussions, and all the other aspects of human information use. We are only now coming to understand the interactions of brain mechanisms, social systems, sign systems, information needs, electronics, art, and luck involved in seeking and using information.

There is no single small set of works to read or rules to follow to fully address the representation of questions and documents. Yet, we must have some starting points. Throughout our explorations, we will pause to consider a few works that establish a setting for our efforts. The works cited in these documents, as well as subsequent works in which the documents themselves are cited, will begin to weave a documentary tapestry of tools for our understanding.

A close examination of the concepts underlying the question "What is it about?" is found in Wilson's *Public Knowledge, Private Ignorance.*[10] Although the text has a copyright date of 1977, the issues remain. Wilson notes: "[W]e may need less information but better procedures for using the information we already have and get." We can also find in this text foundational thoughts on a "reorientation toward the functional rather than the topical or disciplinary."

Buckland addresses the "excitement and unease" caused by the technological revolutions in the infomation arena. He notes, in his *Redesigning Library Services,* that for the "first time in one hundred years we face the grand and difficult challenge of redesigning library services."[11] His elegant model of library services, as noted in this chapter, offers a substantial framework to guide our explorations and keep sight of the past.

It can often be instructive to go over some of the historical materials of a field. Although indexing and abstracting have long been concerns, the approaches suggested in our explorations have their bases in work stemming from the middle part of this century. The nature of that work can be gleaned from several authors. One especially helpful work is the April 1978 issue of the *Drexel Library Quarterly.*[12] Herein, M. E. Maron has gathered works by Wilson, Cooper, Robertson, Harter, van Rijsbergen, and Kuhns, all addressing the theory and foundations of information retrieval. The citations anchor each article in its historical underpinnings. Of course, there were other schools of thought and groups of researchers, but this work still provides a significant focal point.

Bateson's *Mind and Nature*[13] provides one source of thinking about the nature of thinking. Gardner's *The Mind's New Science*[14] supplements works such as Bateson's and provides a good background for the manner in which computers have revivified epistemology. Further considerations of the nature of thinking can be found in numerous works on brain models, such as Minsky's *The Society of Mind*[15] and Churchland's *The Engine of Reason, the Seat of the Soul.*[16] Critiques of machine reasoning are found in the works of Dreyfus, such as *What Computers Still Can't Do.*[17]

Thinking about thinking is critical to understanding representation. Representation is the heart of the matter for us. *Intelligence* by Fischler and Firschein[18] summarizes the work on brain mechanisms of representation, and Marr makes an eloquent statement of the nature of representation in his *Vision*.[19] Blair provides a substantial history of representation, with an emphasis on information retrieval, in his *Language and Representation in Information Retrieval*.[20]

Finally, one would do well to skim through current and back issues of the major journals in information retrieval, as well as communications, computer technology, linguistics, and philosophy. *Journal of Documentation, Microcomputers for Information Management, Journal of the American Society for Information Science,* and *Information Processing and Management* are but a few of the sources of relevant information.

Notes

1. *Doctoral Digest.* Occassional Paper. Berkeley: School of Library and Information Studies, University of California, 1991.

2. Ed Pai designed the model of relationships between a user and a document collection for a paper at the Graduate School of Library and Information Studies at the University of California, Los Angeles. He has since worked with the author to redesign it for the requirements of this text.

3. N. J. Belkin, R. N. Oddy, and H. M. Brooks, "ASK for Information Retrieval: Part I. Background and Theory," *Journal of Documentation* 31, no. 2 (June 1982): 61-163.

4. John A. Wheeler, "Information, Physics, Quantum: The Search for Links," in *Complexity, Entropy and the Physics of Information,* ed. Wojciech H. Zurek (Redwood City, Calif.: Addison-Wesley, 1990), 3-18.

5. After Robert M. Hayes, "Measurement of Information," *Information Processing and Management* 29, no. 1 (1993): 1-11.

6. H. C. Plotkin, *Darwin Machines and the Nature of Knowledge* (Cambridge, Mass.: Harvard University Press, 1994), 16.

7. Marvin Minsky, *The Society of Mind* (New York: Simon & Schuster, 1986); Edward Smith and Douglas Medin, *Categories and Concepts* (Cambridge, Mass.: Harvard University Press, 1981).

8. David Marr, *Vision: A Computational Investigation into the Human Representation and Processing of Visual Information* (San Francisco: W. H. Freeman, 1982), 20.

9. Michael K. Buckland, *Redesigning Library Services: A Manifesto* (Chicago: American Library Association, 1992).

10. Patrick Wilson, *Public Knowledge, Private Ignorance: Toward a Library and Information Policy* (Westport, Conn.: Greenwood Press, 1977).

11.   Michael K. Buckland, *Redesigning Library Services: A Manifesto* (Chicago: American Library Association, 1992), 76.

12.   M. E. Maron was issue editor for a collection of foundational works published in 1978 under the issue title *Theory and Foundations of Information Retrieval*, in *Drexel Library Quarterly* 14, no. 2.

13.   Gregory Bateson, *Mind and Nature: A Necessary Unity* (New York: E. P. Dutton, 1979).

14.   Howard Gardner, *The Mind's New Science: A History of the Cognitive Revolution* (New York: Basic Books, 1995).

15.   Marvin Minsky, *The Society of Mind* (New York: Simon & Shuster, 1986).

16.   Paul M. Churchland, *The Engine of Reason, the Seat of the Soul: A Philosophical Journey into the Brain* (Cambridge, Mass.: MIT Press, 1995).

17.   Hubert L. Dreyfus, *What Computers Still Can't Do: A Critique of Artificial Reason* (Cambridge, Mass.: MIT Press, 1992).

18.   Martin Fischler and Oscar Firschein, *Intelligence: The Eye, the Brain and the Computer* (Reading, Mass.: Addison-Wesley, 1987).

19.   David Marr, *Vision: A Computational Investigation into the Human Representation and Processing of Visual Information* (San Francisco: W. H. Freeman, 1982).

20.   David C. Blair, *Language and Representation in Information Retrieval* (New York: Elsevier, 1990).

Chapter 2

Considerations of
Representation

Representation is a fundamental concept in indexing and abstracting. Most methods of retrieving documents depend on some form of representation of the collection documents, as well as the representations of the questions brought to that collection. The documents put into a patron's hands are a representation of the collection. Although we need not make an exhaustive study of concepts of representation, it will be informative to spend some time considering representation issues relevant to indexing and abstracting.

Representation has already been defined as a system for extracting or highlighting some aspects of an original concept or object, together with some explanation of how the system does this. That is, we have some form of *sign* (in its broadest sense), which is generated from some *original* referent, by means of some *code*. In a general sense, we can say that there is no sign without a code. There may have been a code when the sign was generated, but if any individual encountering the sign does not know the code, there is, in that instance, no sign.[1]

We can put our definition into terms of entities and attributes. *Entities* are the referents or things being represented and *attributes* are the characteristics of the entities. Any object or concept can be termed an entity. The entity can be described as the sum of all its attributes or characteristics. The purpose of the representation will strongly influence just which attributes are highlighted or selected as representative.

The subtleties of the mechanisms of representation remain elusive. Neurologists and artificial intelligence researchers ponder the physical embodiment of information in symbolic forms for use. Philosophers and artists, too, puzzle and argue over how one thing can stand for another. The two following exercises by no means exhaust the nature of representation; they are merely intended to demonstrate two broad forms of representation.

"What Is This?" Exercise

What will be said if we look at figure 2.1 and ask, "What is this?" Most people will answer "a buffalo" or "a bison." Some will say "a buffalo in a zoo." Clearly, however, it is not a bison. If an actual bison were to inhabit these pages, reading this book could be a real adventure. This is a reproduction of a photograph of a bison.

Fig. 2.1. Illustration for "What is this?" excercise.

Similarly, what if we ask of figure 2.2, "What is this?" Viewers who had gone through the preceding exercise might now say, "It's a photograph of some old writing" or "It's a representation of hieroglyphics" or "It's a picture of a stone with writing carved into it." Again, it is not a real stone with carved figures, it is a reproduction of a photograph of a stone with carved figures.

Fig. 2.2. The Rosetta Stone showing hieroglyphic, Demotic, and Greek texts.

What if we ask a different question, such as, "What does it mean?" or "What is it about?" Some might truthfully answer, "It doesn't mean much" or "It's some nice carving." Typically, though, most respondents say something like "I don't know" or "I don't know how to read the text." Even if we add the Greek translation to the hieroglyphics, as in figure 2.3, most people will answer, "I still can't read it" or "It's Greek to me!" or "Isn't that the Rosetta Stone?"

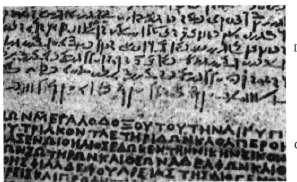

Demotic

Greek

Fig. 2.3. A portion of the Rosetta Stone with the Greek segment shown. The Greek translation of the late Egyptian text enabled translation by scholars, but does not make the text any more evident to the untrained reader.

Direct Presentation of Attributes

The bison image is an example of representation by *direct extraction* of some attributes of the original. Direct extraction of some of the physical attributes enables the making of a sign that stands in the place of a bison. If we wished to show students in a classroom what a bison looks like, we could get a trailer, herd a bison into the trailer, and transport it to the classroom. This might be a valuable classroom experience, but it is not always practical or possible.

If we take some of the animal's attributes, such as color, the two-dimensional shape, and the relative sizes of various body parts, and scale those down to a manageable size, we can bring the essence of bison into the classroom. *Essence* here is defined only in terms of the requirements for the classroom. The essence for a Native American on the Great Plains or a modern-day beefalo rancher would be quite a different matter. Essence might then be in terms of resources available from the animal for food, clothing, spiritual values, or profit margin.

The representation highlights those characteristics suited to the classroom, while leaving out movement in time, size, smell—those characteristics would be inconvenient in a classroom. Of course, a real but dead and stuffed bison might be convenient for some classroom experiences. Yet, even a stuffed animal is a representation; it no longer has organs, or the quality of movement, or the ability to eat.

Regardless of the actual neural mechanisms, this direct-extraction method of representation can be said to be a combination of a sufficient subset of attributes and some form of knowledge that a representation is being made. This combination enables reasoning about the original object or concept and, if necessary, filling in some of the missing attributes.

One term for such representation is *isomorphic,* derived from Greek roots meaning "same shape." Realistic paintings and photographs are prime examples of isomorphic representations. They present two-dimensional projections of the myriad data of an object at one moment in time (usually). Figure 2.4 presents another example of isomorphic representation, with the rule for highlighting (extracting) made explicit.

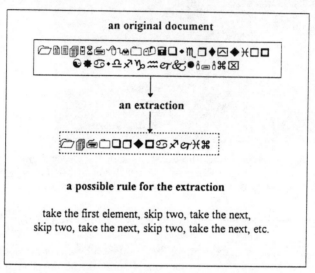

Fig. 2.4. Example of isomorphic representation.

In information retrieval systems, we make isomorphic representations when we provide a small photograph of an art object or a frame from a movie; when we enable patrons to hear samples of a musical selection; when we copy the title as it appears on the title page; or when we put a few works from the collection into a patron's hands. Abstracts that present salient points in words extracted directly from the original article are isomorphic representations. So too are previews for movies and keyword search systems. Photographs and fingerprints in a police database are isomorphic representations, as are audio recordings of speech and music.

Another closely related form of representation can be termed *indexical.* Here the sign is in some way a direct result of interaction with the referent of the representation. Perhaps one of the best examples is a thermometer. The rate of movement of air molecules directly affects a colored liquid in a tube, causing the liquid to rise or fall in direct proportion to the molecular movement. The liquid is not the air molecule movement, but we can tell the amount of movement by the position of the liquid. Other weather-related instruments provide additional examples: the direction of a weather vane; the speed of rotating cups or fins on an anemometer; the outstretched or limp flag on a post.

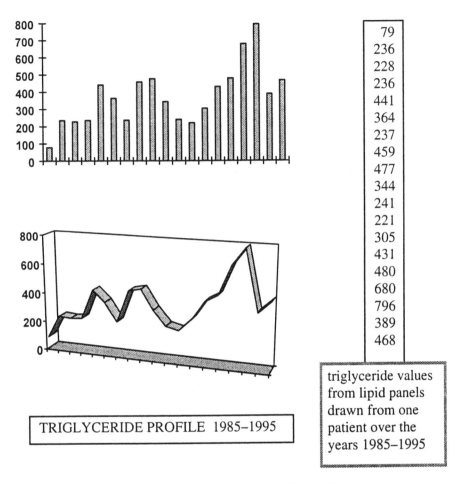

| 79 |
| 236 |
| 228 |
| 236 |
| 441 |
| 364 |
| 237 |
| 459 |
| 477 |
| 344 |
| 241 |
| 221 |
| 305 |
| 431 |
| 480 |
| 680 |
| 796 |
| 389 |
| 468 |

TRIGLYCERIDE PROFILE 1985–1995

triglyceride values from lipid panels drawn from one patient over the years 1985–1995

Fig. 2.5. Graphs are a form of isomorphic representation, as they vary in direct proportion to the numeric values for which they stand.

A bar graph or a pie chart presents a size in direct proportion to the size of some set of numbers or elements, as in figure 2.5. Pebbles used for counting sheep, laps run around a track, or almost anything numerical can be called indexical, because each one represents a given number of items. Even computers use the counting-pebble method when they print a dot on the screen for every "so many" operations in decompressing a file, searching a database, or doing some similar activity.

Photographs can be said to be indexical, in the sense that light bounces off an object, travels through the various mechanisms of a camera, and then directly interacts with a photosensitive emulsion or a magnetic oxide emulsion. This, of course, demonstrates that there is no distinct boundary between isomorphic and indexical representation. It must also be remembered that the direct participation of some object does not necessarily mean a "true" representation. An actor may be made up to look like someone else, or the image may have been manipulated.

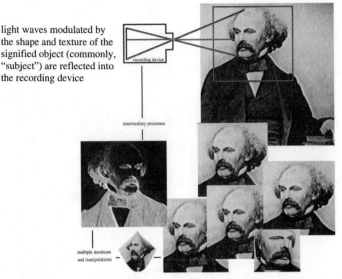

light waves modulated by
the shape and texture of the
signified object (commonly,
"subject") are reflected into
the recording device

Fig. 2.6. Photographing Hawthorne to model the indexical nature of photographic representation.

The direct relationship between an object and a photographic representation of that object is modeled in figure 2.6. A man poses for a portrait. The camera is positioned with its lens aimed at Nathaniel Hawthorne. Light bounces off Hawthorne into the lens and onto the recording medium. Although the picture will be two-dimensional and probably not the same height as Hawthorne, the same relative shapes and gradations of lighting will hold in the representation as in the original.

Indirect Presentation of Attributes

Both isomorphic and indexical representations are *specific*, that is, they are based on individual instances of an object or a concept. Another category of representation forms can be termed *general* because they are based on classes of entities and attributes. They highlight attributes indirectly. Again, we must be careful to remember that the boundaries are not hard and fast between the specific and the general.

A representation may start out based on an individual instance, then become generalized. The photograph of the flag-raising on Iwo Jima is, in one sense, just a representation of a few specific men at a specific moment raising a stick with a piece of cloth on it. Yet, for many, it has been generalized into a representation of the concept of valorous and determined patriotism. The single image of soldiers at one particular moment in history has come to stand for all valorous military acts. *A part is used to stand for the whole.* Such an image can be called *iconic;* it acts as a reminder or a touchstone for a greater web.

Other specific images have come to stand for some larger number of events or concepts. Both the image of an antiwar protester in the 1960s putting a flower into a soldier's rifle barrel and the image of a single man in standing in the path of a tank in Tianamen Square have come to symbolize resistance to tyranny. The picture of John Kennedy's son watching his father's funeral procession evokes all the emotions of the passing of an era.

Of course, the greater meanings are not inherent in the images. They are community constructs. Different communities may well regard the meaning of the images differently. Antiwar protesters might regard the Iwo Jima image as a sad or revolting commentary on blind allegiance to a cause. Many people find the image of the war protester with his flower a symbol of cowardice or treason. Many images that are held by some group to be meaningful beyond the particular instance have no greater meaning at all for other groups.

Photographs are by no means the only sort of iconic sign. Two perpendicular lines (✝) have greater meaning than just two lines for millions of people. This structure and several variations were used in Roman Empire times to execute thousands of people. One execution is held by many to be emblematic of a set of theological constructs. The instrument of one crucifixion out of thousands now stands for Christianity in all its variant forms.

National flags are just pieces of cloth, yet people will give up their lives to keep one from falling to the earth in a battle. People who protest the actions of a country often burn that country's flag. Burning a piece of cloth, in and of itself, has little meaning; burning a flag is taken as a strong statement of "I dislike the actions and beliefs of your group!" During the 1960s, protesters were reviled for wearing flags upside down or with a peace symbol in place of the stars. The image of Abby Hoffman was censored on the "Tonight Show" when he wore a shirt made of a flag, yet one can now go to a sports store at the time of this writing and buy a jacket or shirt printed like a flag. We see that the meaning of the same data set can be different for different groups and at different times.

Some brand names for consumer products come to stand for the class of products. Regardless of the actual brand name or manufacturer's name, facial tissue paper is often called *Kleenex*. Likewise, many people go to their Lanier, or Canon, or Minolta copying machine to do some "xeroxing," although the holder of this trademarked name vigorously protests such usage.

Most people also have iconic images or materials of their own—images or materials for which the greater meaning is known only to themselves or some close group. A rock seen by anybody else would just be a rock with all its general possibilities for meaning—paperweight, sturdy throwing object, and so on. Yet for the individual who picked up the rock during a hike in the mountains with a loved one, the rock can stand for the entire delightful experience surrounding the circumstance of the picking up of the rock. A minuscule part of the event can bring back the sights, sounds, smells, physical sensations, and emotions of the entire event.

Arbitrary Trace

Moving along a spectrum of the sign's distance from the original, we come next to the *arbitrary trace,* or what we might call a *sign by agreement.* In the picture of Hawthorne in figure 2.6, we have a sign standing for a man, which sign was made with the direct participation of a particular man. Without going into various linguistic theories, we can say that there is little or no direct connection between the lines **MAN** and some individual male member of the group *Homo sapiens.* We have agreed that a certain sound will stand for the general concept "man" and that we can have certain signs stand for that sound and concept. Different groups may develop different signs for the same (or similar) concept. *Andros, homo, man,* and *homme* are different sets of lines used by different sets of people to stand for the same concept.

Even when we label specific elements of a group, there is no direct connection between the sign and its referent. The man in the image in figure 2.6 is the author Nathaniel Hawthorne. Nothing about the shape or size of these letters that stand for his name derives from that individual.

Even when an individual writes his or her own name (for example, Hawthorne's signature in figure 2.7), the only connection is that that person physically made the trace. This may make the trace valuable or more meaningful for some people, but it does not make the trace resemble that person any more.

Wittgenstein suggests that groups create verbal tools for use in conducting their lives.[2] People living where it snows frequently have numerous terms for different types of snow, whereas people in equatorial regions may have no term at all for snow. This makes sense. Whether you are hunting for food, devising shelter and clothing, operating a ski resort, or planning to travel by car, you want to know if the snow is light and fluffy, dense, mixed with sleet, or hard-packed. In an area where there are earthquakes, people will have concerns for the distance from the epicenter, the type of ground motion, the time separating the component waves, the soil type in various locations, and the time of day. To those watching television news in a state other than California, "a moderate earthquake struck the San Fernando Valley today" is sufficient.

Most Sincerely Yours,
Nath.' Hawthorne

Fig. 2.7. Hawthorne's signature. The signature, like the photograph, is a representation generated with the direct participation of the signified object. However, it is mediated by a code that removes it from any resemblance to a direct experience of the object.

The important thing to realize about the arbitrary trace in terms of information retrieval is that, in Wittgenstein's terms, the map is not the territory. People need to know the agreed-upon sign system; otherwise, "It's Greek to me" will be the feeling. Also, different people will likely make different uses of the map. A book in French given to a person who does not read French will be no response to a question, regardless of how appropriate the concepts in the document might be. Even a document in the patron's native tongue will be of only limited utility if it assumes knowledge of a discipline or literary style that the patron does not possess.

For our concerns with indexing and abstracting, we must be especially concerned with three aspects of representation:

- purpose as it influences mode of representation

- no representation without a code

- synchronic and diachronic attributes

——————————Purpose and Mode of Representation

Constructing Representations of Unfamiliar Objects: An Exercise

An exercise in representation will help to make some of the points of our discussion more immediate. This works well with a group of people, but it can be adapted by the single reader. In a group, oral presentations with demonstrations or drawings are the usual mode; an individual might want to take a walk and do the mental exercise of describing observed items. It would be most useful to do the exercise described here before continuing with the remainder of this chapter.

Assume a situation in which a disparate group of objects must be described to someone who cannot ask questions or make suggestions. Perhaps this is an archaeological expedition making a video report of its findings from the previous week. Gather together a group of items and assign one or two to each team of three or four people. Unusual items and pieces of ordinary items make the points strongly, but ordinary items can be just as meaningful. Give the teams 15 minutes to examine the items and prepare a presentation. It is important not to influence the manner in which the presentation is made or what its contents might be. Simply say something such as: "Report on your findings."

Items in a recent "archaeological dig" included:

- a piece of denim with a button with the symbols "I Love NH"

- a book with the cover title "Catulli Carmina"

- a one-inch hemisphere of rubber

- a four-inch diameter, three-wheeled object with visible electronics, but no words

- a reel of computer tape with "Marty" handwritten on the case

- a plastic container with an electrical cord but no moving parts

- a paper bag with lamp wire, switches, a socket, a switch, and a lightbulb

- a videocassette with no label
- a two-inch stone
- coin-size circular pieces of plastic in several different colors
- a twelve-inch long, one-inch diameter cloth tube
- an empty compact disc carrying case

Brief Discussion of Exercise. The two elements common to nearly all of the reports will be a *description of the physical attributes* of the item and some *description of purpose* or speculation about a possible purpose. The purpose descriptions may range from "We just couldn't figure out what it could be used for," to something rather close to the intended purpose, to bizarre and extraordinary speculations. Physical attributes and purpose will be the dominant concepts common to all forms of representation.

Representation History of a Familiar Object

An interesting progression from a specific representation to a general representation that we use every day can be started with the image of an ox in figure 2.8. Suppose we lived some 3,000 years ago and had reason to transport the idea of an ox to some distant place (perhaps to the royal accountants). As with the previous bison-in-the-classroom example, we could bring the real beast, or we could bring some representation that would be adequate to the needs of the accountants. Perhaps a drawing of the head, as in figure 2.9, would be sufficient.

horn

ear

eye

snout

Fig. 2.8. Photograph of head of a bison, which can be included in the family of animals termed "ox."

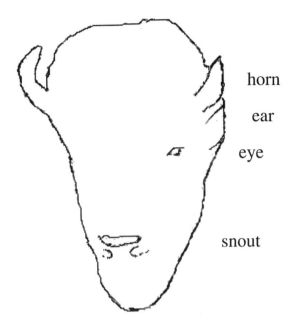

horn

ear

eye

snout

Fig. 2.9. Sketch of ox head with outline of basic shape and parts.

We have here the roughly triangular shape of head and snout, two small shapes jutting out where ears would be, and projecting arcs where horns would be. The rest of the body is left out, the color is left out, odor is left out, movement is left out—yet the remaining parts suffice to carry the idea of an ox.

Suppose now that we have to make an image for each one of a hundred or more oxen. It might seem reasonable to reduce the number of strokes and to simplify the remaining strokes. An image such as that in figure 2.10 still has the basic shape of head and snout, ears, and horns, but the irregular contour has been simplified to three simple (albeit intersecting) arcs.

An increased need for speed or simplicity could yield a sign such as figure 2.11. Here the head, ears, and horns have been reduced to straight lines forming a triangle with projections of the line segments. The basic shapes and orientations of parts remain the same. The general concept of an ox remains.

Over time, others may wish to use the representation we have developed for *ox,* but they might not be so careful in their design construction, and might orient the basic shape in some other manner, as in figure 2.12. They may also come to regularize the production of the shape, as in figure 2.13. Also, they may just want to use our sign for *ox* to remind them of the sound of our word for *ox.* They do not need to convey the idea of a whole ox, but they want to remember sounds, perhaps for a religious ceremony of some complexity.

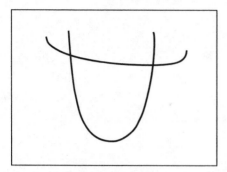

Fig. 2.10. Simplified sketch of ox head.

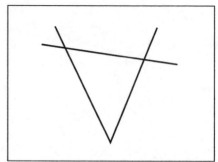

Fig. 2.11. Further-simplified sketch of ox head.

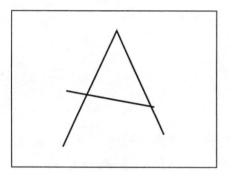

Fig. 2.12. Symbol for sound of *ox*.

Fig. 2.13. Romanized version of Greek symbol.

In a crude retelling, this is the development of our letter "A." The letter "A" in the Roman alphabet (here in a Times New Roman font) still retains a hint of the essence of ox, even if upside down. The progression from a specific representation of an animal or other object to a letter parallels the progression from orality, through the occasional use of signs for a few specific purposes, to a general alphabet. The alphabet is a simple code system capable of great complexity in its output. Both the simplicity and the consequent complexity are the result of generality. It is no longer required that there be an individual sign for each and every object or concept or even class of objects or concepts.

The actual nature of the progression—from crude marks to signs to letters—is still under debate. Did Mesopotamian accountants and other officials develop the ideas over a long time period and keep the secrets to themselves? Did the idea arise essentially full-blown and spread rapidly among a large group? The scanty evidence is tantalizingly adequate to support either direction of theorizing, but inadequate to prove either. Whichever way the progression took place, it is interesting to note our direct linguistic ties to the animals of the Mesopotamian region. The term for ox from that region is *aleph*. When that was transformed by the Greeks into the sign for the sound we recognize as "A," the word was slightly transformed into *alpha,* from which we derive *alphabet*.[3]

Sign and Code

There is no sign without a code. We mentioned this concept earlier and we saw in the preceding exercise that in the absence of a code we are left with guesswork. It is common in discussions of this concept to mention sign systems from cultures of some other time or place. "It's Greek to me!" means we do not have the code and can make no more sense of the sign than that it is intended as a sign.

Until the Rosetta Stone, with its Greek translation of hieroglyphs, was discovered, Egyptian writing was just so many squiggles, even to Egyptologists. Painted and carved marks on stones in the American Southwest are obviously the work of humans, but in most cases we do not have the code and cannot decipher a meaning.

Libraries present a more immediately vexing example of the concept "no sign without a code." It is quite likely that success will elude the patron who does not know that the Library of Congress Subject Headings are a mode of representation; that they are applied at the level of the document; and that questions must be translated into these terms. The code for tagging concepts is not made explicit. Even well-educated, frequent users of the library are often unaware that there is a system of subject headings.

More troubling is the idea that we do not make explicit to users of information systems just how the salient concepts were determined. Especially in systems where only two or three concepts are selected to represent the whole document, this failure presents a major roadblock to successful searching. Even the patron who is familiar with the subject headings or classification scheme in use in a particular setting has no way of knowing how some other person extracted the "main" concepts of the document.

Even in machine-indexing environments, the patron can be at a considerable disadvantage if the rules for extraction or ranking are not made known; if the contents of a stop list (those words considered meaningless and, therefore, not ranked) are not made known; if any uses of synonymy or translation or generalization are not explained.

If the means by which the system accomplishes its highlighting are not made known, the representation is not complete. If the concept-tagging system is not made known, the representation is not complete. The patron is left in a position of having signs without a code. However, the situation is more insidious than that of the archaeologist faced with squiggles from another time and place. The patron is hampered by the "illusion of knowledge."[4] The system is not obvious in its failures. Indeed, it may even work well with sufficient frequency that the patron who cannot find something assumes that the library just does not have anything that would be an appropriate response. In reality, a document might well exist in the collection, but the patron lacked sufficient knowledge of the code used to represent that document.

Synchronic and Diachronic Attributes

Attributes of document entities are the focal point of a related course of discussion. As we pointed out in the archaeological exercise, descriptions of an object usually include both the observable physical attributes and the purpose of an object. We can link this to two broad categories of attributes:

Diachronic—those that remain the same across time

Synchronic—those that may change with time and place

These are closely linked to the concepts of:

Physical text—the marks or squiggles, whether on paper, stone, videotape, or other medium

Conceptual text—the concepts generated in any individual user by the squiggles

"Hamlet" will always have been written by Shakespeare. "I can't get no satisfaction" will always be a phrase in the song "Satisfaction" by Richards and Jagger. "Arma virumque cano" will always be the opening of the *Aeneid.* Instruments playing a Beethoven symphony or Stravinsky's *Rite of Spring* will always set air waves into motion in the same way. These are *diachronic attributes,* the physically present text.

Not everyone will understand all the concepts within "Hamlet" with the facility of a Shakespeare scholar or a theatergoer of the author's time. Many parents, teachers, and clergy were upset with the sexual innuendo and rock music of "Satisfaction," but many people delighted in both the music and its expression of sexuality. Years later, the song seems simplistic in its orchestration and tame by comparison in its sexual expression.

"Arma virumque cano" was the opening of a work that was important and compelling in its time; today, relatively few people pick it up to read, and those who know of it often have dreadful memories of high-school Latin class. Beethoven and Stravinsky were not always held in high regard. The Paris opening of *Rite of Spring* evoked considerable revulsion. These differences in reaction to the same squiggles are the *synchronic attributes,* the conceptual texts.

Not long ago, one could not say "pregnant" on television; today, many sexual topics and practices are presented on network programming. Words for which Lenny Bruce was ostensibly harassed by authorities are common fare on cable comedy shows. Less dramatic but just as exemplary are all the gender-specific pronouns in works created well into the 1970s. Even scholarly works frequently said, "How is a man to . . . ?" or "If anyone . . . , he. . . ." For many readers and viewers today, though certainly not all, these cause hesitation about use of the document. The worth of the document may not be significantly diminished, but the question arises: "How could the author say that?"

In older movies, horses were tripped with wires in stunt scenes; in a time when animals were regarded as expendable, this was acceptable to audiences. Now films with animals often carry a statement of compliance with regulations for humane treatment. An astronomy book for children written in the 1950s suggested that "men" would go to the moon sometime in a rocket ship, but not in the lifetime of the reader. For many of the readers, this is now simply not true. In nineteenth-century art and writing, it was popular to display women as ethereal and saintly by virtue of illness and victimization; today, this is not acceptable to many.

The number of examples of changes in synchronic attributes is large indeed. It would be an interesting exercise to take a few moments and jot down more examples of changes. Changes in the way television commercials are produced, or editing pace in movies of 20 years ago, or music enjoyed by different groups of people, or reactions to documents by persons of different political persuasions are but a few of the areas to be explored.

In library and information management, we have become quite good at making use of diachronic attributes. If a patron can supply a title, or author, or publisher, or even a date, we can do a good job of retrieval. However, we have not been good at providing access by means of utility, especially concept as defined or evaluated by each patron. This is not to say that this does not exist at all. Reference librarians or reader's guide librarians often give evaluative representations of documents based not only on their own beliefs but also on the reactions of other patrons to the documents. There is also the practice of putting some sample of works into a patron's hands, saying "Here are some things that might work for you," then going to find more like those the patron has found most useful.

We would not be in error, though, to say that information retrieval is still based largely on the diachronic attributes of documents. We do not account for the author's stance or "slant" on a topic; we do not account for the reactions of various groups of patrons; we do not account for current validity of the data, assumptions, or conclusions; we do not account for the knowledge base required to make use of the text.

Also, we do not often inform the patrons that we do not account for the synchronic attributes. We do not tell them that indexing is not usually tailored to individual or small-group requirements, perhaps with the exception of special libraries and research collections. Again, by not presenting a major aspect of how the system accomplishes its highlighting, we are compromising the integrity and utility of the representation.

People coming to the document collection with information requirements *do not know something.* This means that they may well have difficulty formulating the proper signs to express concepts. If I take my car to a mechanic because there is "sort of a scrunching sound when I release the brakes," I am in a difficult position. If I do not know anything about calipers, or idler arms, or all the other arcana of automobiles that might relate to a "scrunching sound," satisfactory results may come only at great expense.

If I go into a furniture store looking for a chair to go with a particular look I have in mind, but I have no knowledge of the technical terms for types of chairs or names for different periods, all I can say is, "I need a chair." Then the salesperson will have to conduct an interview and perhaps show me some samples to narrow down the size of the category *chair.*

If I move from an urban area in California to a small town in Kansas and go to the ranch store to buy winter clothes, I may be faced with a bewildering array of boots and cold weather gear. It all looks western and it all looks substantial, but I have little idea of what sort of boots are intended for what sort of use. I may not want to appear ignorant or out of place, so I puzzle in solitude over heel shapes and sizes, toe shapes, type of leather, and insulation, as well as the construction and appearance of coats and coveralls.

Tools in Search Space

Our purpose, the codes with which we are familiar, and the situation in which we find ourselves all work together to determine how we come to find and understand signs. These may be spoken language, objects in our surroundings, or documents in a collection. It is vital that we account for these attributes of any user who comes to a retrieval system. Presenting the diachronic attributes—the physical text—or even the synchronic attributes of one person—the indexer or abstractor—at one particular point in time may not be sufficient to the user's needs.

Representations act as the tools to reduce search time and search space. If the tools are to be useful, they must be suited to the task. We would not use a sledge hammer to drive in carpet tacks and we would not use a carpenter's hammer to crack sections of a concrete sidewalk. A garden hose is useful for watering plants, washing the car, and cooling off children in the summer. It can be used for brushing teeth or putting out a house fire, but only with great difficulty.

Our considerations of representation are intended to aid in the construction of suites of tools capable of providing each patron with an appropriate level of engagement with the document collection. To fashion such tools, we have to consider the nature of the tasks to be accomplished. We must examine:

- The nature of documents and their use

- The relationships between users and authors

- The concept of a subject of a work

- The components available to construct tools suited to individual purposes

Indexing and abstracting have been the primary tools for accomplishing the goals we are considering. We will examine the components of such representations and consider how they might be adjusted and refashioned to be the most useful tools possible.

Notes

1. Umberto Eco, *A Theory of Semiotics* (Bloomington: Indiana University Press, 1979).

2. See, for example, the discussion by D. C. Blair in the chapter "Language and Representation: The Central Problem in Information Retrieval" in his *Language and Representation in Information Retrieval* (New York: Elsevier, 1990). Pages 143 to 155, in particular, discuss Wittgenstein in relationship to semiotics and other systems for studying signs.

3. For an in-depth discussion of letters in history, see Johanna Drucker, *The Alphabetic Labyrinth: The Letters in History and Imagination* (London: Thames & Hudson, 1995).

4. S. Weisburd, "The Spark: Personal Testimonies of Creativity," *Science News* 132, no. 19 (1987): 299. Weisburd quotes Daniel Boorstin: "The obstacle to progress is not ignorance, but the illusion of knowledge."

Chapter 3
Representation and Utility

Representation can be situated within the context of recorded documents and their use, as in figure 3.1. Such a *context web* indicates the numerous points at which issues of representation enter into the relationship between an individual with an information requirement and an individual document. The following discussion focuses on each element of the model in turn.

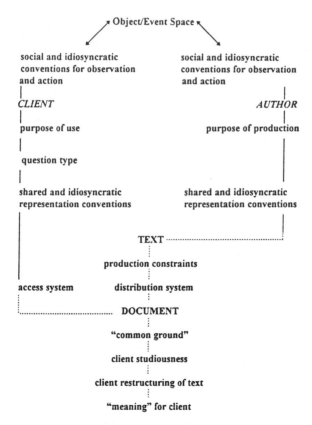

Fig. 3.1. Representation context web.

Object/Event Space

Setting aside some of the intricacies of physics and philosophical considerations of just how we experience the world around us, we can posit an *object/event space*. All the particles in the universe are subject to certain forces and thus hold certain relationships to one another. Segments of this set of relationships can be termed *objects*. These relationships may change over time. Changes in the relationships among the particles over time we will call *events*. This is especially the case for changes viewed by a particular aggregate of particles that would commonly be considered a sentient being.

Of course, different viewers may select different chunks of particles and name and use those chunks differently. The same viewer at different times may choose to select a different configuration of particles holding some subset of an earlier group and use a different name. A quote attributed to Buddha suggests this chunking for use:

> In the sky there is no east and west. People create distinctions out of their own mind and believe them to be true.

Similarly, artificial intelligence pioneer Marvin Minsky noted that humans are quite capable of making more than one use of the same chunk:

> How would you classify a porcelain duck, a pretty decorative toy? Is it a kind of bird? Is it an animal? Or is it just a lifeless piece of clay? It makes no sense to argue about. . . . We frequently use two or more classifications at the same time.[1]

Regardless of how any individual or group clusters the elements of the universe and makes use of them, and regardless of how we might say we know the universe about us, we can say that we each deal with the world on a daily basis and throughout our lives. Each of us operates within many arenas and many roles. The range of our activities is great, as we:

- contemplate the morality of actions toward others
- change diapers
- drive to work
- view the stars overhead
- mow the lawn
- compose music
- weed the garden
- consider humanity and its place in the cosmos
- generate models of land mass movement
- practice dribbling a basketball
- smoke bees from the hive and gather honey
- worry about a date for the prom
- write stories about the San Francisco earthquake
- consider electronic funds transfer across borders

- worry about government budget cuts
- look for the car keys
- panic over lost files in the computer
- seek a physician for our child's pain
- decide where to eat lunch
- give aid to those who have no lunch
- examine background radiation for clues to the beginning of the universe
- buy smoke detectors
- write books and make movies
- take the dog for a walk
- wonder if sentences are too long

All of our actions and interactions, both realized and potential, we will call the *object/ event space.*

——————— Conventions of Observation and Action

Each person grows up within a web of beliefs, customs, language structure, political and philosophical paradigms, and circumstances requiring action. The education system, of whatever sort, shapes each person's way of viewing the world, yet individual circumstances may lead to individual variation. That is, we each bring a similar physiological set of tools to our observations, but there are small variations in our abilities and experience that may yield significant differences. Also, each of us experiences group situations (such as school) in different ways. Each of us has abilities to consider and remodel the things we have learned in social settings. We can critique, compare, judge, and contemplate alternatives.

Authors and users of their works each have a set of conventions. If the author of a work and a potential user share backgrounds, their conventions are likely to have significant overlap; if they do not share backgrounds, the degree of overlap will be smaller, perhaps approaching very little or none.

If I read a book on indexing and abstracting written by someone who studied with some of my own mentors, the familiarity is high and even the novelty is situated within known material. Of course, if the level of familiarity is very high, then I might not want to take the time to engage the book, as I likely know most of the material. If I read a book on evolutionary epistemology by a British author, then the familiarity with the topic is modest but the language conventions are reasonably familiar. If I read a French treatise on semiotics, then language conventions stand in the way of my full engagement if I do not read French fluently.

If I read the works of Homer with the aid of a dictionary, then I can gain some of the insights from a time long since past. However, I can have only a halting understanding of what it would have been like to be a part of Attic Greek culture, to feel the necessity of oral poetry, the belief system, or the political environment. I can study cultural artifacts and make assumptions that help me increase my common ground with the author, but it will never be really high.

Author and Client

Author here is taken in the broad sense of its Latin root to mean anyone who causes a work to flourish. This might be a writer, painter, filmmaker, composer, editor, librarian, teacher, or programmer, among others. Certainly, there are authors of more ephemeral messages, but the primary material of our field is the recorded message. *Client* is taken in a generic sense to mean anyone who comes to any document collection seeking to resolve a knowledge gap. Payment, position, time spent in the collection, and level of system help required have nothing to do with the definition. Other terms are used more or less synonymously— user, seeker, patron.

In the preceding model, figure 3.1, the author and the client are shown making their separate observations of the world about them. These two views are compared in the "common ground" stage near the bottom of the model. Here the degree of congruence between the author and the user is established. The client may make a decision as to whether the overlap is adequate. Such a decision may well depend on the urgency of the information need. If the document is to satisfy casual interest, it is unlikely that finding a translator or immersion in a different culture will be contemplated. If, in contrast, it is necessary to know a work in a foreign tongue to complete a doctoral dissertation, then time and energy simply must be made available for that purpose.

Purpose

Some of the decision about the adequacy of the common ground, then, is dependent on *purpose*. Pratt suggests that the majority of reasons for constructing a document or for consulting a document can be summed up in four categories:

Motivation—try to get the reader excited about an idea or cause

Articulation—try to make evident the workings of a concept

Education—try to pass on useful skills or methods of thinking and doing

Felicitation—try to entertain[2]

Of course, these are not necessarily distinct categories. The same user may seek two or more at the same time. The same document may be able to serve different purposes for different users.

Question Type

Also linked to the determination of adequacy is the *question type* with which the client comes to the system. Broadly, we may distinguish between simple (though not necessarily trivial or easy) data requirements on the one hand and two types of complex requirements—topical and functional—on the other. Data requirements can be met by a single (or small set of) responses about which there is little or no doubt. This does not necessarily mean that finding a response to a data requirement will be easy or that such questions are in some way trivial. However, the evaluation of rightness and completeness is simpler.

Data requirements are easily defined and the results are evaluated simply. If I need to know the name of the wife of the fifth president of the United States, I can be reasonably certain that there is a correct response. If I need to know the mean distance between the earth and the moon, I can be reasonably certain that there is only one figure. If I need to know the species of birds generally seen in Kansas, then I would expect a list with quite a few names. However, this would be shorter than the list of all birds. It might be that some such lists would be a little longer or a little shorter than others. These differences would be the result of differences in observation practices or constraints of time, money, or space on the production of the list. They would not likely be because of fundamental differences in how to define a bird that is seen in Kansas.

Topical and functional requirements both relate to more ill-defined regions of a patron's cognitive maps. Searching and evaluation are required. The time and place and paradigmatic foundations of a work come into play. As an extreme example, we might safely opine that few astronauts today would want to base a trip to the moon on a pre-Copernican text of the solar system. We may find, however, that although there is a great deal of literature on post-Darwinian concepts of the animal world, many people base their relationships to animals on a pre-Darwinian model.

Within this more diffuse form of information requirement, we can identify different types of questions. *Clearly articulated questions* are those in which the patron knows what is needed, though its exact nature may not be describable. For example:

- I need just enough about the Gulf War to give a talk at the Kiwanis Club next week

- I need to know how to build a deck onto the back of my house

- I want to visit sites painted by French Impressionists

- I need information to help me decide when to have my first baby

These are not trivial retrieval tasks, but the judgment as to utility is reasonably easy to make.

More difficult to operationalize is the *vague awareness* that there is a need for information. Questions of this sort constitute a form of seeking in which the patron says, "I am not sure what I want, but I'd know it if I saw it." We may have to bring together pieces of information from numerous disparate sources to satisfy questions such as:

- I am having difficulty relating to my teenage son. Where should I look for information?

- I am not satisfied with my financial situation. How do I go about making changes?

- What do I need to know if I have to determine mainstreaming policies for autistic children?

- Why should we preserve documents?

- What should I read to understand the possibilities of expert systems for reference?

"Monitoring the information environment" and "shaking up the knowledge store"[3] both acknowledge a different form of information requirement. They are activities carried out by those who say "I know I don't know everything." Professional people, artists, and scholars know that information is constantly being generated and that some of it may be useful or vital, even though it is not nominally within a particular discipline or topical subject heading.

Monitoring the information environment ranges from checking tables of content in a wide variety of journals, to surfing the Internet, to browsing the new book shelves in the library. There is no stated goal, only a reasonable likelihood that something useful will be recognized if seen.

The phrase "shaking up the knowledge store" was coined by the Intrex Conference to refer to all those activities undertaken when a person goes looking in no particular place for something that will put a new twist on an idea, bring two distant ideas together, or stimulate a new train of thought. This may take such forms as random browsing or finding a license plate number and using it as a starting point in a classification scheme or purposely going to a section of a collection that has nothing to do with one's own ideas, job, or discipline.

Conventions for Representation

Just as people have conventions for observation and action, so too they have shared and idiosyncratic conventions for representation. These include not just language, but also the use of language: epic poetry or personal narrative; political oratory or talking blues; encyclopedia entries or historical fiction. It might well be argued that the place the novel once held has been taken over by film and video; that the making of one's own music has been supplanted by CDs and personal tape players; that children's fiction-making has been dislodged by easy access to videotapes for repeated viewings. We can look to the television commercials of the 1960s and see not only peculiar fashions and products, but also crude production techniques. Films that seemed compellingly new and different in the 1970s now often seem ordinary or passé because the production techniques were incorporated into mainstream production and then surpassed.

Of course, we can also look to circumstances in which there is little sharing of conventions for insights. Again, "It's Greek to me" comes to mind. We do not have the convention of either oral poetry (with such exceptions as talking blues, rap, books-on-tape, and story hour) or the Greek poetic language. Few of us today would sit through the dozens of hours required to recite the *Iliad*.

We can, though, sense a little of the strain between difffering conventions of representation. Every generation's parents seem to complain about the raucous noise that children call music these days. The difference in camera angles, editing pace, and lighting between *Miracle on 34th Street* or *Dr. Zhivago* and MTV is in a similar vein.

Such differences in representation codes are always an issue for authors, regardless of medium. The balance of the familiar and the novel is always crucial. Does one throw caution to the wind and throw something totally new at the audience (for example, *Rite of Spring* or performance art in the grocery store), or does one just push the edges a little bit, so that the larger audience is likely to go along?

These differences are also important in our considerations of information retrieval. The patron who has to struggle with the mode of presentation may not feel that the effort is warranted, or may misunderstand the text, or may make the effort only to find out that there is little of value in the document. Of course, it is possible that an unfamiliar method of representation will prove extremely compelling and revelatory for a patron. The very mode of presentation may make the material all the more evident.

Text and Document

Somehow an author makes a decision on what slice of the object/event space to consider and for what purpose and by what means. Although there is still considerable dispute on the nature of authorship, text, and reader, there are some important generalities. We must first think of the difference between what the author (again, regardless of the medium) has in mind—here called *text*—and what actually ends up in the hands of the patron—here called *document.*

The author may have a great idea, but not have the money to realize it. The author may have a great idea, but simply not have the craft to mold the chosen medium to realize the idea. The author may have a great idea and skill and money, but not have time or access to needed material. We may refer to these as *production constraints.*

Constraints are also established by the distribution system. Just what topics are considered salable or appropriate can determine whether a document, regardless of its potential value to some individual, ever makes it to market. The decision to distribute the work in a different medium from the original can further restrict or increase the distribution. Constraints might also include reviewers and any competitions or promotions by which recommendations and purchase decisions are made.

Part of the distribution system includes any decisions by a library or bookstore or video store on how to display and promote a product. Wear and tear on documents as they are used by more and more people is an aspect of distribution that must be considered. In the electronic environment, the issue of access time as a function of number of users constitutes a similar concern. We might also include the information workers who decide not to purchase certain works or to purchase large numbers of certain works. We could also include any direct manipulation of the work, such as putting labels on the working part of a diskette, or cutting out pictures of nudes, or accidental ripping of pages, or purposeful corruption of a file.

Such actions can mean that the piece that ends up in the hands of the patron is not a perfect reproduction of the author's original concept. Nevertheless, it is from this *document* that issues of common ground will be decided and from which the patron will gain whatever is to be gained.

Studiousness

Studiousness speaks to the resources of time, intellectual effort, and physical effort a patron is willing to commit to finding a satisfactory resolution to the information requirement.[4] The desirable solution might be seen as never having a need to go to a document collection in the first place. Next to this ideal, being shown the one or few works that will suit the need well seems to be desirable—low studiousness.

Generally, only the person with a compelling problem or a professional position dependent on information is willing to do a great deal of searching and evaluation. Even within a single work, a user may seek only certain portions, rather than engaging the entire piece.

This is, of course, quite reasonable in some circumstances. A work may be of use only in part, so why should one expend additional resources? We may say that the user participates in constructing the meaning of a work by restructuring the work. If you subscribe to a weekly news magazine, such as *Time, Newsweek,* or *U.S. News and World Report*, it is unlikely that you read each and every word of each and every page in sequence from beginning to end. You have favorite segments, other segments that you generally skip over entirely, and still others that you check on occasion. Probably you read an editorial or cartoons or letters and then go on to other regions.

Meaning and Utility

All of these interactions, conventions, and considerations come together at the point where the user derives some meaning from a document. The word *meaning* is even more diffuse than many of the others we have considered. We might simply say that *meaning* is the change or reinforcement made to a user's set of models of the world after engaging a document.

Indexing and abstracting help a patron to locate meaningful documents. Just as the meaning of those documents depends on conventions, codes, purpose, and studiousness, so too do indexing and abstracting. It is difficult to overemphasize the importance of the concept that meaning and utility depend on the coding system and a user's decoding ability. We will take some time now to work through another example of form and utility.

If purpose drives the selection of attributes for a representation, then it is reasonable to assume that a particular form of representation determines what one can do with it. Our purpose, of course, is to maximize the utility of question and document representations. However, a simpler example may make clear the notion of utility of a representation.[5]

If I had some horses and wanted to let somebody else know how many I had, I could pick up a rock or stick for each horse, or I might draw a line or dot for each one.

* * * * * * * * * * * * * * * * * *

This is reasonably convenient as long as I do not have more than several dozen animals. If I do have a larger number of animals, I need a sign system that reduces data; I need a system that provides a single sign for some larger number. One example of such a system is Roman numerals. These give me a shorthand system for constructing large numbers.

XVII

Here the *X* stands for ten, the *V* stands for five, and each *I* stands for one. The sign for our number is more compact. However, there is a significant problem with this method of representing numbers. The absence of a place-value system makes manipulation of numbers difficult, if not impossible. There is no convenient and systematic method for multiplying or dividing. Once a number is known, it can be represented, but there is no inherent method for calculating a number.

The introduction of a place-value system and a zero to stand for the empty place enabled complex manipulation of numbers. In the common decimal system, 10 digits are used over and over in positions that multiply the digits by some power of 10. This results in the "ones, tens, hundreds, thousands" system learned in elementary school. In such a system we can represent our number of horses with economy of pen strokes:

17

We can also determine a profit margin if we have 17 horses that cost $7.13 each for feed and shelter for a month and after six months 8 new horses have been born and at the end of two years we sell all but 2 at $535 each. Elementary-school-level activities can calculate the profit of $8,369.24 in this rather idealized example.

We could make 17 piles of pebbles, each with 713 pebbles, to stand for the number of pennies required to provide for the original group for one month. We could then duplicate this five times, for a total of six groups of 17 piles each with 713 pebbles. The same sort of process could then be repeated for the 25 horses over 18 months. We could then make 23 piles to represent the 23 horses sold. Each of these piles would have 53,500 pebbles. Then we could take away all the pebbles in the cost pile one by one, at the same time taking from the profit pile an equivalent number of pebbles. The remainder of the profit pile would represent our gain in pennies. Roman numerals would offer only a marginal improvement. We could label each small pile and each larger pile, but we would still have to do the counting.

Computers use only two states to perform functions—off and on. This means that a 10-digit system or a system of any other number of digits (except 2) is not suited to implementation in a computer. A binary system will work, though. Here "1" and "0" represent the "on" and "off" states. Place values are still a part of the representation, with each position representing a power of two. Our sample number—* * * * * * * * * * * * * * * * *, XVII, 17—would look like this:

10001

That is, reading from right to left:

- there is a "ones" (2^0) value of "1"
- there is a "twos" (2^1) value of "0"
- there is a "fours" (2^2) value of "0"
- there is an "eights" (2^3) value of "0"
- there is a "sixteens"(2^4) value of "1"

1 times 1 = 1; 2 times 0 = 0; 4 times 0 = 0; 8 times 0 = 0; 16 times 1 = 16
1 times 1 = 1 16 times 1 = 16
TOTAL = 17, * * * * * * * * * * * * * * * * *, XVII

If I wish to indicate the sounds associated with our number, I can type *SEVENTEEN, seventeen,* or *Seventeen,* or I can handwrite the equivalent letters. In figure 3.2, we can see that a binary code—American Standard Code for Information Interchange (ASCII)—enables a computer to represent the alphabetic *seventeen,* as well as the numeric concept.

ASCII Values for SEVENTEEN & seventeen

alphabetic (decimal)   binary place values

	64	32	16	8	4	2	1
S (83)	1	0	1	0	0	1	1
E (69)	1	0	0	0	1	0	1
V (86)	1	0	1	0	1	1	0
E (69)	1	0	0	0	1	0	1
N (78)	1	0	0	1	1	1	0
T (84)	1	0	1	0	1	0	0
E (69)	1	0	0	0	1	0	1
E (69)	1	0	0	0	1	0	1
N (78)	1	0	0	1	1	1	0
(32)	0	1	0	0	0	0	0
s (115)	1	1	1	0	0	1	1
e (101)	1	1	0	0	1	0	1
v (118)	1	1	1	0	1	1	0
e (101)	1	1	0	0	1	0	1
n (110)	1	1	0	1	1	1	0
t (116)	1	1	1	0	1	0	0
e (101)	1	1	0	0	1	0	1
e (101)	1	1	0	0	1	0	1
n (110)	1	1	0	1	1	1	0

Fig. 3.2. Decimal and binary representations of the word form of "17."

So, pebbles or other items used for one-to-one correspondence are convenient and still have utility, even in a digital environment. A system such as Roman numerals reduces time in representation and looks good on statues and other formal objects (according to some folks). A system such as arabic numerals maintains economy and adds manipulability. Ones and zeros sacrifice some economy in representation, but in an electronic environment they enable rapid manipulation well beyond human capability. Visual representation of the associated sounds works well in formal writing and looks good on a magazine cover.

—— Form of Representation in Information Retrieval

The context web for representation is of fundamental importance to indexing and abstracting because, ultimately, the success or failure of a search may hinge on one representation. The user will have only the tool that is offered as the interface between a knowledge gap and a collection of documents. If that tool does not account for the elements of the context web as they relate to a particular patron, the representation has a high probability of being useless.

The utility of a form of representation is a crucial element of information retrieval. Just as in the example based on the number 17, the form of representation determines what sorts of tasks can be accomplished using the representation. Title representations are, in a sense, analogous to the use of stones to stand for the number of items in a group. The title is extracted directly from the document. It stands for the whole document. It may or may not give an immediately evident clue to the contents. If a patron knows the title of a work, the search is a data search presenting little, if any, difficulty. If a patron does not know the title of a work that can answer the information requirement, the title is of no use as a finding tool. If the patron can guess a title word, and the title word reflects the contents, and the patron has access to an electronic environment or a knowledgable reference librarian, the title may well be of use. If the user applies a synonym of the title word to the information requirement, in many cases, the title is of little use.

Subject headings stand for concepts but do not necessarily use the elements of any particular document to represent the concepts. This brings together similar documents that may use differing elements of expression. This collocation can be useful to many patrons, yet it is achieved at the cost of requiring knowledge of a secondary code. The patron must translate the query concept into system terms, that is, the same subject heading that was applied by the system.

Elements, such as keywords, extracted directly from the document offer a search tool made of native elements. A patron need not translate the query; however, works using synonymous elements can easily be missed, unless an additional layer of representation (e.g., a thesaurus) is included in the system.

The level of generality from which the representation is drawn also determines the utility of the representation for any given user. Representation at the level of the whole document will hide smaller but still significant components from users. In contrast, either the patron or the system must expend additional resources if representation is carried out at deeper levels of generality. Patrons looking for works "largely about" a particular topic do not want to have to wade through a lot of details.

—————————————— Utility and the Code

We can say that a representation works only to the degree that any user knows the code and to the degree that the code is capable of embodying useful elements and proceedures. Again, there is no sign without a code. The utility of a sign depends on the coding system coding something worthwhile. That is, just because a patron knows the coding system does not mean that unimportant material properly coded will become useful.

Purposeful obfuscation by choice of representation offers another way of considering the utility of representations. It has been suggested that copyright dates on films were done in Roman numerals to make it more difficult to determine when the copyright period expired. Leonardo da Vinci used mirror writing to enable the keeping of notes while reducing theft of intellectual property. Spies and school students devise codes so that messages can be sent over distances and yet be of value only to those who have the code.

The type of representation chosen can clarify or obscure the message for certain readers. Perhaps these instances of the necessity for transmission of concepts are especially useful for getting to the heart of representation. Some set of symbols or traces are devised to stand in place of objects, concepts, and activities. For those who have the code, the objects, concepts, and activities are decipherable (the pictures are regenerated in the recipient's head). For those who do not have the code, the squiggles are meaningless. They are not signs; they are not representations.

Notes

1. Marvin Minsky, *The Society of Mind* (New York: Simon & Schuster, 1986). See page 91 for the quotation and for a discussion of "Levels and Classifications," that is, how humans may well hold the same object in several different classifications according to requirements of use.

2. Allan Pratt, *The Information of the Image* (Norwood, N.J.: Ablex, 1982).

3. C. F. J. Overhage and R. J. Harman, eds., *Intrex: Report of a Planning Conference on Information Transfer Experiments* (Cambridge, Mass.: MIT Press, 1965).

4. Patrick Wilson, *Public Knowledge, Private Ignorance: Toward a Library and Information Policy* (Westport, Conn.: Greenwood Press, 1977). See especially pages 94 to 99, but read the surrounding material for context.

5. David Marr, *Vision: A Computational Investigation into Human Representation and Processing of Visual Information* (San Francisco: W. H. Freeman, 1982).

Chapter 4
Indeterminacy and Depth

The subject of a document is not some creature that inhabits the work. We cannot simply shake the document and have it drop out, self-evident to all who gaze upon it. At this point in our explorations of the representation of questions and documents, we will enhance our critical perceptions by putting ourselves into two roles, first that of patron and then that of indexer. We will build on what we have covered so far; we will also lay some of the groundwork for subsequent discussions of access models that are responsive to individual requirements.

Exercises in Subject Representation

Exploration of the sense of subject and the difficulties one may encounter by assuming a single entity—"the subject"—will be aided by engaging in two exercises. Each puts us in a role on one side of the actual representation. The first exercise has us confront the use of representations already generated by somebody else. The second has us generate representations with others in mind. To facilitate the conduct and analysis of the exercises, the procedures for both tasks are presented together. The analyses for both follow. It is strongly suggested that you conduct the exercises before you read the discussions.

Exercise One

Listed in this exercise are several questions for which there ought to be resources in a modest academic library or even a large public library. In a classroom setting, it might be desirable to divide the questions, perhaps three to a person. A search period of one hour should be allocated. Obviously, if a patron desperately needed material, a search might be protracted beyond 20 minutes per question. Nevertheless, one hour for three questions is not an unreasonable approximation of the time that a patron or an intermediary would allocate to a first search.

A search form template follows the questions (fig. 4.1 on page 50). This form will facilitate discussion of strategies, results, and consequences. Making notes of false leads, seemingly good hits that turn out to be marginal in value, and serendipitous findings is a valuable activity here. Keep in mind Cutter's suggestion that an access system ought to enable a patron to know what materials a collection has on a certain subject.

Before you set off on your search, you should note that these questions are asked in the manner that a real patron might present them to a reference librarian or other search intermediary. They are all of the class that in chapter 3 was called "well articulated." The patrons are reasonably sure of what they want and there is not a great deal of ambiguity inherent in the majority of the questions. It is, however, possible that the questions are not "properly" stated. A question implies a lack of knowledge of some sort. Therefore, it is possible that the state of ignorance constrains the construction of the question.

Of course, some of these questions could become passé, or responses to some of them may become common knowledge. It should not be particularly difficult to generate more questions of a similar sort. Indeed, it would be a good secondary exercise to generate a set of similar questions and discuss the characteristics of the questions.

Search Requests

- My father-in-law was a world-class gymnast. He has a substantial lay interest in artificial intelligence. He is now wondering about robotics and gymnastics, particularly tumbling. What do you have available on tumbling robots?

- What information is available on the relationship between photography of the American West and the engravings by Remington on the West?

- Why do translations of Homer's works contain the phrase "wine dark sea"? Is this an error in translation? Does it have something to do with ancient Greek perceptions?

- What role did librarians play at CNN during the Gulf War?

- Where can I get detailed pictures of the inside of a space shuttle?

- I am interested in pilot training and I understand that there's a book about using trampolines to do some of the physical training of pilots. Where is that?

- Is there a video or part of a video portraying medieval troubadours?

- Are there any personal accounts of vacationing on any of the islands off the New England coast, particularly any associated with New Hampshire?

- I would be interested in contemporary accounts or project reports on machine systems for browsing developed in the 1950s or 1960s.

- I have a collection of antique glass lantern slides that I would like to put into a computer. Are there any magazine articles or books that could give me some hints about the techniques of actually getting them into the machine and, maybe, how to think about organizing them?

- What is available on radio as an art form?

- I've heard there is a good book on animal tracking written by a former hunter who is now a vegetarian. Can you help me get hold of that book?

- There is a lot of talk about paradigm shifts these days. Has anybody come up with an algorithm for determining when a paradigm shift took place or predicting when one will take place?

- Are there any articles on the difficulties of achieving sense of touch on the skin (other than fingers) in virtual reality?

- Where might I find accounts of prison life by first-time, nonviolent offenders?

- With all the talk about space shuttles and space stations, I was thinking about all the pictures they must take. Are there any articles on automated processes for indexing all these pictures?

- Every once in a while in the library school I hear the name *Hipacia*. Is this a place, an acronym, a company, or a person? Are there any books or videos about whatever it is?

- I need some examples of Carolingian manuscript.

- Are there any newspaper columns or anything like essays that were written by the woman who wrote *Little House on the Prairie*?

- How did the Romans send messages and military dispatches around their empire? Did they use anything like mirrors or fire or carrier pigeons?

- Do you know of any videos or parts of videos that demonstrate the method of casting type for printing?

- Since most physicians, until recently, were men, is there any misogyny in medical illustration, especially before 1980?

- Is cold fusion still the subject of research anywhere?

- Where can I find some reviews of Blake's *Representation and Language for Information Management*?

- It seems to me that with all the interest in artificial intelligence, somebody in philosophy, or some area like that, must have given consideration to the potential for revitalizing epistemology. Can you be of any assistance to me?

- The movie *Desk Set* seems to have to do with the information profession. Is there some information about the relationship this film has with actual librarians, database management workers, and other information professionals?

- Are there any speculations on what might have happened in the world if steam power had become prominent in transportation, communication, and computing?

- Where should I begin looking for material on representation as it relates to vision?

- What is a good text for learning about evolutionary epistemology?

SEARCH FORM

Searcher name: **Date:**

Question:

Search strategies:

Terms:
     Initial:

     Revised:

Candidate works:

Works found (with evaluations):

Comments:

Fig. 4.1. Search exercise form.

Exercise Two

Simply find an article of modest length, say 4 to 10 pages. Each person involved in the exercise should then index the article. To the question, "What do you mean by indexing?," the answer should be, "Indicate ideas in the article which you could imagine someone would be happy to find." There are no constraints on number of terms or form of presentation. The exercise should take only half an hour.

The article used as a sample here is "The Vindolanda Tablets" by Anthony Birley from *Minerva*. Vindolanda is the site of a Roman fort with a "remarkable state of preservation of the finds, especially a collection of legible writing tablets which have provided a unique insight into the daily lives of soldiers in this Roman fort close to Hadrian's wall." The article details the history of the fort, the excavation of the site in recent years, and the techniques of observation and preservation. Photographs present a collection of shoes, a woman's hair piece, numerous writing styli, and actual written messages. Mention is made of birthday invitations and a contractor's invoice from the site. Quotations are given from letters dealing with daily life at the fort, including one with a curious familiarity: "I have sent you . . . pairs of socks from Sattua, two pairs of sandals and two pairs of underpants. . . . Best wishes to Tetricus and your mess-mates, with whom I hope you are living in the greatest happiness."[1]

After indexing is complete, it is most instructive to display all the terms devised by everyone engaged in the exercise.

Discussion

Again, the subject of a document is not some creature that inhabits the work. Rather, the *subject* is a relationship between each individual and the squiggles that constitute the document.[2] If the subject were a single, self-evident entity, then subject representation would be only a slight challenge. We would need only to list the synonyms that reflected differences in terminology. In reality, most documents have a good many squiggles. The circumstances of the patron and the nature of the squiggles combine to generate a unique, user-dependent meaning for each engagement with each document.

Of course, the meanings that are generated will generally (but by no means always) be within bounds that are, to some degree, predictable. One would not expect to learn how to grow vegetables in Kansas from a book on evolutionary epistemology, nor how to make a mid-life job transition from a book on tiger sharks. Yet, there remains a large range of possibilities.

It is only an incidental consequence of packaging that the documents in a collection of any sort are individual entities of a particular size. So far as a patron is concerned, all the data in a library or electronic database is one large document. Just where the information for a particular requirement resides is of little consequence. That we generally point to (index) or summarize (abstract) information at the level of the document is a matter of system convenience, not a reflection of minimum useful size of an information package.

Discussion of Exercise One

The difficulty of finding substantial and useful subjects embedded within larger documents is one of the primary points intended to be made by the first exercise. In a large collection of documents with a paper-based card catalog, the difficulties of filing and maintaining even a small number of cards for each book could be enormous. One reasonable solution has been to represent the document at the level of the whole document; that is, do not worry about the details, just represent the most general topic.

However, as should be evident from exercise one, a considerable wealth of material may be hidden from users by not providing for topics at a greater level of detail. Several of the questions in the exercise were designed to make this point.

- Tumbling robots are the subject of chapters in an annual review of artificial intelligence from MIT. Nothing in the title or the Library of Congress Subject Headings for the book suggests tumbling or robots. In fact, no title of a chapter mentions tumbling. The term *gymnastics* is the closest to tumbling. So, to find these chapters, one must generalize from tumbling to gymnastics, and from robot to artificial intelligence, and then look for works on artificial intelligence that would be broad enough in coverage to include robots. Even then, one would have to go through several works on artificial intelligence to find the specific topic of gymnastics. Alternatively, one could think of institutions where there is considerable activity in artificial intelligence and robotics and look for publications from those institutions, then go sifting for gymnastic robots.

- A small section in Arthur Zajonc's *Catching the Light* (New York: Oxford University Press, 1993) deals with Homer's use of "wine dark sea." However, nothing in the subtitle, table of contents, or subject headings points to Homer. To find this material by a subject heading search, one must generalize to the idea that color is an attribute of light and that philosophical or physiological considerations of light might be a subject under which to search. Then one still has to go through the index of each work (at least) to check for Homer.

- The librarians at CNN are the subject of a small portion of General Perry Smith's book about CNN and the Gulf War (*How CNN Fought the War*, New York: Carol, 1991). Again, nothing in the subtitle, subject headings, or table of contents indicates that this material is to be found within.

- A Navy pilot training manual from the World War II era has an extensive section on the use of trampolines for training pilots. Once again, there is nothing explicit in the standard forms of representation for access to indicate that trampolines are discussed within. If one knew that Keeney, one of the authors, was an expert on trampolining, one might look for works with his name. This would be too much to expect of most searchers.

- James Burke's *The Day the Universe Changed* television series contains a segment on the changes wrought by the printing press. Within that episode, there is a dramatization of troubadours as information transfer agents of their time. There is no evidence of this in the title. One could only guess that the time period likely to be covered by a consideration of printing would also include troubadours.

- Rezendes's *Tracking and the Art of Seeing*, cited in the preface of this book, is written by a former hunter turned vegetarian and wildlife photographer. The only aspect of the document that mentions the author's being vegetarian is the introductory material.

- Personal accounts of prison life by first-time offenders can be found, among other sources, in a book about protesters during the Vietnam conflict era. Once again, one must generalize quite a bit to find this work. It is possible to find works on prison life through Library of Congress Subject

Headings. However, this book is not entirely, or even largely, about prison life, so it does not have a subject heading reflecting prison life.

- Artificial intelligence and the revivification of epistemology is the topic of Howard Gardner's *The Mind's New Science* (New York: Basic Books, 1985). Here, epistemology is not explicit in the representations, though one might expect that anyone who would ask such a question could connect the term *philosophy*, which does occur, with epistemology.

Two of the questions in the list were designed to elicit consideration of the nature of a question, even when the information requirement can be articulated reasonably well. The question about Hipacia will not go very far in most systems because of the spelling. The patron has heard the word, but can only guess at the spelling. Just what sort of entity a hipacia might be is unclear, so the appropriate search paths are unclear. The more generally accepted spelling—Hypatia—would make things simpler. There are speculative novels about this woman, as well as some historical fragments. Perhaps the best retelling of her story is found embedded in a few lines of the Sagan work, *Cosmos* (New York: Random House, 1980). Here the name appears in the index, though it is not a subject heading for *Cosmos*.

Similarly, the question regarding the book by Blake, entitled *Representation and Language for Information Management*, will cause problems for most systems. The patron has gotten the author's name confused and has muddled the title. If this were not the case, the search would be trivial. If the patron searches by author name or by title, there will be no retrieval. If a reference librarian or a "what to do when there are zero hits" screen on an on-line catalog suggests trying alternate spellings of the author's name, Blake could become Blair—perhaps. In an electronic environment, there might be a suggestion to try a title word search, in which case "representation" and "language" would point to *Language and Representation in Information Retrieval* by David Blair (New York: Elsevier, 1990). Presumably, the patron would assume that this must have been the item sought. Yet that assumption is based on some sophisticated knowledge about human abilities to confuse spellings and word orders. It is also based on the patron knowing of the possibility that the original question might be stated incorrectly.

The question about steam power raises an issue about system representation of the collection as a whole. One of the most eloquent speculations on this topic is in the form of a novel—William Gibson and Bruce Sterling's *The Difference Engine* (New York: Bantam, 1991). Fiction works present a great deal of material that could be responsive to information requirements, yet access has generally been very limited. Usually author, title, and genre constitute the totality of access points.

Discussion of Exercise Two

A general pattern of response has arisen from several iterations of this exercise in the past. A major portion of those indexing compile lists of 5 to 10 terms, whereas another group compiles a list of considerably greater length. Many who have worked in libraries or used them frequently will attempt to construct terms in the manner of Library of Congress Subject Headings. Several will ask "Can we use xxxx?" or "Is it all right to mention xxxx?"

Most notable about the exercise is the number of terms derived. Even articles of four or five pages generally have 50 to 100 terms in all. Remember that the instructions simply said to list elements that some user might be happy to find. Many elements of only minor consequence within the framework of the article might still be of considerable interest to someone. For example, if I were writing an article on women's hair fashions, I might be quite interested to know that the Vindolanda article mentions a hairpiece from nearly 2,000 years ago and that a photograph is available. Perhaps, if I were preparing an advertisement for a word processor, I would be interested in Roman fountain pens that still worked. If I were writing a dissertation on handwriting and representation, I would surely want to know of early examples of daily communications. The list of terms in table 4.1 is typical of the results from conducting this exercise with the Vindolanda tablets article.

Table 4.1
Results of Group Indexing of "The Vindolanda Tablets"

archaeology	archaeology, Roman	artifacts
writing tablets	Britain, Roman	soldiers
fort	Hadrian's wall	boots
daily life of soldiers	shoes and slippers	hairpiece
styli	wattle and daub walls	excavation
preservation	Vindolanda	coins
stable flies	natural defenses	[all place names]
[all personal names]	stone fort	fort-village
camp followers	traders	anaerobic conditions
chamfron	leather objects	army tent
handwriting	handwriting, Roman	vulgar Latin
fort family life	"little Brits"	birthday party invitation
Roman army society	Roman army economy	letter to soldier
infrared photography	garrison	stylus tablet
filing	fountain pens	conservation techniques
site laboratory	stylus tablet	socks
underpants	sandals	[photographs]
army, ancient Rome	papyrology	Roman soldiers
conservation, leather	writing utensils, history	conservation, leather
Roman handwriting	iron nib pens	Latin
Rome—1st cent. AD	Britain—1st cent. AD	Latin—vulgar
pens, iron nib	metal objects	spear heads
needles	rings	environments, ancient
Latin, use of	Roman clothing	cohort of Tungrians
horse chamfrons	buildings, history, Roman	British heritage
Celts—history	archaeology, sites, Britain	Rome—0–299AD—forts
historic ruins	timber forts	artifacts—restoring

As we look at these typical results of a group exercise in indexing a single article, we can see some questions implicit in the variety of terms. Within these questions, as listed in the following, the term *element* has been substituted for *word*, so as not to exclude image and sound documents. What is made evident from the exercise with a word-based document might be applicable to documents in other media. The insights can be summarized as:

1. Just how many elements should be extracted?
2. Which elements should be extracted?
3. Should the elements be extracted in their natural form or translated?
4. Should the elements be in a natural order or a constructed order?
5. Should generalization of individual concepts take place?
6. What are the rules to guide extraction?

If the indexing is to be a representation, then we can say that not all the elements in the document will be used. Yet, beyond this limiting case, we must ask whether there is some ideal raw number or ideal percentage of the total number of elements in the document. Then we ought to refine this question by asking "ideal for whom"? If we speak of an ideal system for those who must manage it, perhaps one or two elements would be the most economical use of resources. However, if we mean ideal for the patron, we may have to assume a much larger number, at least in some circumstances.[3]

Closely associated with the number of elements to be extracted is the issue of which elements to pull. In word-based documents, we might well say that words such as all forms of the verb "to be," most prepositions and articles, and pronouns should be considered to hold too little meaning potential to be included in the representation. What additional constraints could we add? Assuming we want to be liberal in providing access, we have to consider the balance between enough and too much. That is, where is the balance between high utility and inordinate use of time? Is the balance point the same for all users? Is it a sliding point dependent on user requirements? Is some golden mean available?[4]

We must further consider just what the elements will look like when presented to the patron. Are the salient elements from the document simply to be extracted and put into some useable order? This would seem to ensure the closest relationship between the document and the representation.

However, if the words are professional jargon or from an author from a different time or place, they may not be sufficiently familiar to be useful. The patron might not be able to guess that these are the sought terms and might not understand them even if they are found. It is also possible that the author has used several disparate terms for subordinate concepts, but has not represented the more general concept well.

One alternative to direct extraction is the use of a sanctioned list of terms through which all extracted terms are translated. This brings together synonyms and other disparate codings for similar concepts. Of course, one has to hope that differing concepts or differing levels of concepts are grouped together in an understandable and useful manner. The sanctioned list (such as the Library of Congress Subject Headings or the ERIC Thesaurus) must provide access to the accepted term from all the possible terms it translates.

An interesting variation of the indexing exercise involves the direct use of a thesaurus. Following the same beginning steps, restrict the terms that can be used to those found in a sanctioned list. Comparing the terms derived by all the various participants can be most instructive. Each person should explain the translation process from the extracted term to the sanctioned term.

If we are dealing with word-based documents, should we use natural word order or inverted word order for the representative terms? Should we argue that people typically want to find the general class first and then move down a tree of hierarchy to the specific concept they seek? Just which is the more general concept: Archaeology or Roman or Great Britain?

If we seek anything "archaeological," then "Roman" and "Great Britain" are secondary partitions of the greater concept. If we seek anything about Rome (poetry, politics, statuary, etc.), then "archaeology" is a subset. If we seek historical material or travel guide material about Great Britain, then "Roman" and "archaeology" are the detailing partitions. Should we provide for multiple configurations of the same set of concept tags?

If we choose to extract terms directly from the document, what then of higher and lower degrees of specificity? That is, do we depend on the elements of the document to present their own hierarchy of relationships of concepts in the document? Need we construct generalized or more specific terms if these are not provided? If we move beyond word-based documents, can we assume that individual elements will be adequate to express levels of generality without some additional context?

Finally, are there any real rules beyond "Read the work and you'll know what the subject is"? Even if we say that an indexer is to use a certain number of terms and to think about what terms would likely be used by patrons who would be happy to find the work being indexed, can that be considered enough? Are there other rules that would ensure that any indexer looking at the same work would generate the same representation? If there are such rules, would machines not be nicely suited to indexing? Are rules to ensure uniformity really what we want if different users have different needs and decoding abilities?

Subject Representation

Our two exercises raise the possibility that there is frequently a wide gulf between the tools generally provided for access and the requirements of the persons using those tools.[5] The exercises present two primary questions:

1. Why was it hard to find so many of the documents needed in the first exercise, when they were available?

2. Which parts of a document does one choose, and how ought one to present them?

One significant part of a response is presented in figure 4.2. It is not the necessary case—but it is a frequent case—that the patron is largely or completely left out of the representation process. Some external party—here termed the *bibliographic agency*—establishes the rules by which documents are represented, the rules by which questions are represented, and the rules by which the two representations are compared. The individual patron does not have an opportunity to input what coding/decoding abilities he or she has. The patron does not get to specify the depth of penetration into the collection or the individual documents. The patron is seldom told just what the rules of highlighting are in the system of representation being used.

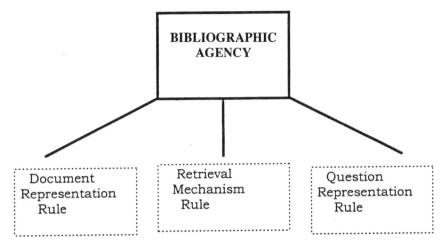

Fig. 4.2. Model of typical representation by agency.

Of course, most indexing and abstracting does not take place in total ignorance of or disregard for the likely patrons of the system. For example, if the language of the user community is English, then most of the documents will be in English and most of the representation will be in English. Academic libraries, specialized databases, and special libraries will probably be staffed by persons familiar with the content area and the specialized clientele. This may lead to closer attention to appropriate terminology and deeper levels of detail.

Yet, there remains the troubling fact that there is little formal inclusion of the patron in the representation process. If the system does not take the user's decoding abilities into account, it cannot be said to use a code known to the user. Thus, it is only by chance that a proper sign—a true and useable representation—is generated.

Notes

1. Anthony Birley, "The Vindolanda Tablets: Roman Writing Revealed," *Minerva* 11, no. 2 (February 1990): 8-11.

2. M. E. Maron, W. S. Cooper, and S. E. Robertson, "Probability of Relevance: A Unification of Two Competing Models for Document Retrieval," *Information Technology: Research and Development* 1, no. 1 (1982): 1-21, especially page 4.

3. M. E. Maron, "Associative Search Techniques Versus Probabilistic Retrieval Models," *Journal of the American Society for Information Science* 33, no. 5 (1982): 308-10.

4. Charles T. Meadow, *Text Information Retrieval Systems* (San Diego, Calif.: Academic Press, 1988);

5. David Blair, "Indeterminacy in the Subject Access to Documents," *Information Processing and Management* 22, no. 2 (1986): 229-41. The entire article deals with the topic of subject indeterminacy and its consequences.

Chapter 5
Representation and the Formal Bibliographic Apparatus

The exercises in chapter 4 helped us to elicit some of the difficulties posed by searching with the typical tools of the formal bibliographical apparatus.[1] We now consider formal models of those difficulties, giving special attention to the issues of representation. The discussions use indexing as the focal activity, but, on the whole, they relate to most of the forms of representing questions and documents, such as indexing, abstracting, classification, reference interview, and database design.

The general model, presented as figure 4.2, hints at the reasons for some major difficulties. Nothing in the model prohibits the bibliographical agency from providing ad hoc representation based on rules suited to the individual patron. However, such a system requires considerable resources and cleverness.

Representations that are going to stand as is for some time can only present the diachronic attributes of the document—those that do not change. Author, title, publisher, date, spine height, and length are attributes that can be extracted without any consideration of the patrons at all. Subject headings too can be constructed without consideration of the patrons: Simply tell the indexer to come up with a few terms that he or she feels describe the topic of the book. If these work for a patron, fine; if not, it cannot be helped.

Of course, many who provide subject representations do try to take into account the general nature of the patrons using the system. Yet there are no formal rules requiring such consideration. Even if there were such rules, we might ask just how accommodation of the patron would actually work.

Let us step back for a moment and ponder indexing. Basically, three modes of indexing are available:

1. Human examines document and extracts or applies terms.

2. Machine examines document and extracts or applies terms.

3. Machine makes preliminary pass; human refines terms.

Obviously, the machine is only following rules made up by humans, but the crucial point is that the human programmers had to make precise rules. The rules are followed for each and every document. One could expect that the same program running on several different machines would produce the same representation of the same document. Research shows that one cannot make the same assumption about human indexers. Indeed, one cannot even assume that the same indexer will represent the same document in the same way at two different times.[2]

This is because humans generally act on gut feeling or some assumption that if they read the work, they will know what the topic is. There is even some evidence to suggest that humans attempting to follow an algorithm will not index in precisely the same way because of the vagueness and vagaries of language.

We discuss machine-assisted representation in chapters 7, 8, and 9. For now, we can say that a machine-based system of representation offers consistency in application of rules. Also, those rules, whether or not they are made evident to the user, are at least available to the system managers. Of course, consistency in the application of rules is a positive attribute only if the rules provide useful retrieval.

Cooper suggested that indexing consists of "great vagueness and much generality resting on a foundation of shifting quicksand." These rules for representation typically used by human indexers speak only to diachronic attributes and only to structural aspects of the process of subject representation. For example:

1. Use direct content—that is, index only what is actually in the document.

2. Cutter's rule—index at the whole document's level of specificity.

3. System constraint on depth of indexing—e.g., use only three terms.

There is nothing inherently wrong with saying "index only what is actually in the document." Indeed, a great deal can be gleaned from counting words. However, as our discussions of representation point out, "what is actually *in* the document" can be said to be a function of both the document *and* the user.

Cutter's rule was an attempt at a rigorous process of representation. However, it took only a few examples from the exercises in chapter 4 to show that it is not sufficiently rigorous to accommodate a heterogeneous user group.[3] In a sense, Cutter's rule can stand for the whole class of problems that arise when there is a discrepancy between the needs of the patron and the system's method of representation.

Subject indeterminacy is the phrase proposed by Blair to stand for this class of difficulties. We will examine Blair's model by first suggesting that, within the general model presented in figure 4.2, several implied assumptions must hold true for the system to provide satisfactory results. Subsequent figures present various scenarios in which not all the assumptions are valid.

Document

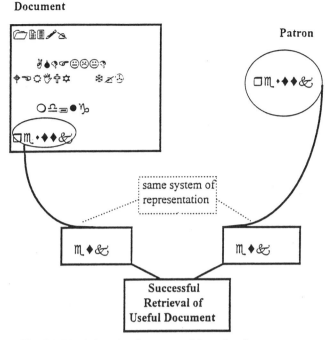

Fig. 5.1. Ideal situation for successful retrieval.

The scenario modeled in figure 5.1 is the ideal situation, in which all assumptions hold true. Here we are considering only one document. An individual patron has an information need that would, in fact, be satisfied by the document in question. When the person constructing the representation (e.g., indexer) examines the document, she or he must select the concept that will satisfy the user. This may be at a very general level or at a very specific level. The user may have no idea whether there is a whole document devoted to the information need, or just a paragraph or two. Whatever the circumstances, the concept that will help the patron must be the one selected by the indexer.

The user must be able to articulate the concept. The user must be able to put that articulated concept into system terms. That is, if the system is based on the Library of Congress Subject Headings, then the concept must be presented as a Library of Congress Subject Heading. This assumes that the patron has some level of facility with the system.

The person making the representation is, presumably, skilled in the use of the particular system for representation. However, it is quite possible that there is more than one way to code a particular concept, even within a particular system. In many cases there will be links (such as "see" and "see also" references), but there is no guarantee that such links will exist. A person looking for information on the history of military installations in Great Britain might not immediately think of "Roman army—forts," for example. Of the candidate possibilities for the description of the target concept, both the patron and the indexer must select at least one in common.

Document

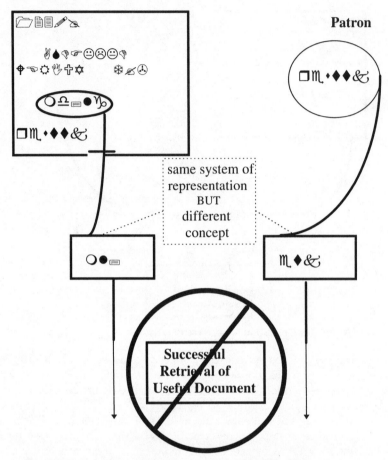

Fig. 5.2. Failure due to difference in concept identification.

It is quite possible to imagine that the indexer and the patron are both skilled in the same system of representation, but the indexer, constrained to select only some small number of concepts, selects one that will not satisfy the patron, as in figure 5.2. The concept is in the document, but it is not highlighted. The patron who depends on the representations in the system will bypass this document.

It may well be that another document will be found within the system. That document might have a reference to the bypassed document. In this case, the document can be found. However, in terms of the current search, the representation fails. Without user input at the time of representation, the system does not know what elements ought to be highlighted.

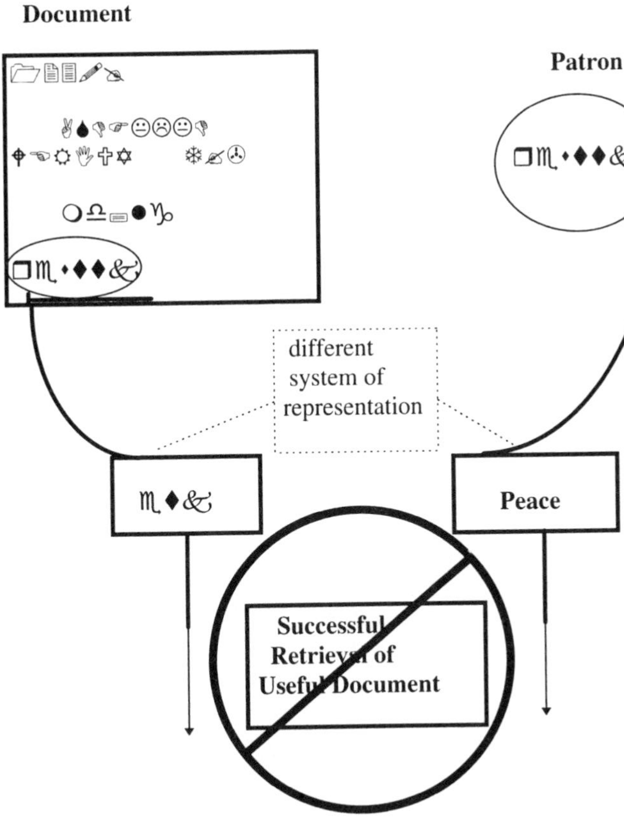

Document

Fig. 5.3. Failure due to difference in representation systems.

In figure 5.3 we see another common scenario. Here the patron is not familiar with the system of representation being used by the system, although the patron may be familiar with some other system of representation. For example, a person accustomed to using a computer to search by keywords in titles might have little idea of how to operate within a system using Library of Congress Subject Headings. In the former system, the patron can just think of a word and see if there is a title containing that word. In LCSH, the patron must guess at a complex string of words, which may have nothing to do with any word in the title. One can also imagine patrons accustomed to the way commercial audio retailers arrange compact discs being unable to operate within a Dewey Decimal audio collection.

Even if the patron and the indexer identify the same concept, the representation will fail because the patron has not been made aware of the rules. Of course, if there is sufficient time and interest, the patron may receive some bibliographic instruction (or the equivalent in an electronic environment). It may also be that the patron will seek help from a system employee, essentially to translate from one terminological system to another. If the patron does not know the coding system, there is, for that patron, no sign, and thus no representation.

Document

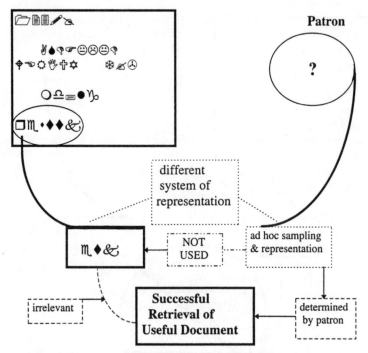

Fig. 5.4. Successful search without use of formal system.

In the preceding scenarios there has been an assumption that the patron can give at least some vague idea of the information requirement to the system. However, what are we to make of the case of the artist or scholar attempting to generate new knowledge? The system cannot make even a guess at which concept in a document would be useful to such a patron; even the patron cannot articulate the information requirement.

The generation of new knowledge requires, at some critical point, the finding of new connections, new twists, new observations. If it is the "new" that is sought, then, by definition, it cannot have been identified yet. Therefore, it cannot be a subject heading. In such an instance, as in figure 5.4, the very idea of the system providing representation is meaningless.

There may well be value to representing documents for other patrons, but the potential generator of new knowledge has no need of it. Later on in the process, the formal bibliographic apparatus may come back into play to provide "more things like this." However, the nature of the search has then changed.

For decades, academic librarians have puzzled over the fact that engineers, physical scientists, humanities scholars, and social scientists have made little, if any, use of the formal bibliographical apparatus. If we acknowledge that the apparatus is set up to answer topical queries, and that scholars need functional information that they cannot articulate until it is seen, there is no mystery about this nonuse.[4] If there is no way of stating which elements ought to be highlighted, then there is no way to design a representation system in advance of use.

Browsing is the activity or set of activities used by scholars to get around the difficulties of representing documents in advance of use by searchers with no clearly stated goal. We consider browsing in greater depth in chapter 6. For now, we can say that *browsing* is a willful putting aside of the pointing and summarizing functions of indexing and abstracting, and a recognition of the wisdom of going through each and every document. Of course, such recognition does not generate more time for searching.

The browser takes a different approach to representation of the collection as a whole. If there is no articulated question, then each and every document is just as likely to produce a useful response. The searcher might want to exclude documents that are already known, such as those normally associated with the searcher's discipline. Equal likelihood of satisfaction means that the browser can make a random selection of documents. The rule for what to highlight is "anything," or "anything I have time and energy to put my hands on."

Once a document is found, the method of examination and subsequent moves, both within the document and within the whole collection, are determined by the browser. That is, once within some point in the collection, the representation changes from "anything" to "everything I know to any degree, in my terms of understanding." Figure 5.5 presents this scenario of elimination of third-party, a priori representation.

Document

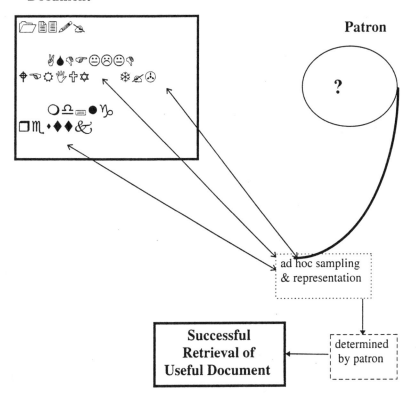

Fig. 5.5. Browsing as idiosyncratic representation.

Depth of Indexing

Closely related to the preceding scenarios is the concept of depth of indexing. Cutter suggested representation at the level of the whole document. There are, however, often useful elements at levels of greater specificity. There are two sorts of depth to be considered:

- The number of descriptors for any one document
- The conceptual detail represented by the terms

As an aspect of representation, this should seem self-evident and worthy of rather little special attention. Essentially, we are talking about which elements to highlight and the ability of the descriptors to discriminate between concepts at the document level and within the document.

However, two other concepts related to depth have been made important measures of system performance. *Precision* and *recall* are numerical ways of stating the degree to which a search has succeeded. The concepts are useful, though in practice they are very difficult to achieve.

Precision is a measure of the gems-to-trash ratio. That is, of all the documents put into the patron's hands, how many are actually useful? *Recall* is a measure of just how many of the useful documents in the collection actually end up in the patron's hands. Both measures are usually expressed as a ratio or percentage. See figure 5.6 for definitions. Clearly, what we would like to see are high values for A (rightly put into patron's hands) and D (rightly left out of patron's hands). This implies that we would like to see low values for B (wrongly put into patron's hands) and C (wrongly left out of patron's hands).

As the framework for some examples, let us assume that we have a collection of 20 documents and that we have the means to know which documents satisfy the patron, as well as which of all the documents could have satisfied the patron.

	useful	not useful	total
in patron's hands	A	B	A+B
not in patron's hands	C	D	C+D
total	A+C	B+D	A+B+C+D (whole collection)

PRECISION = A / A+B   RECALL = A / A+C

Fig. 5.6. Precision and recall as measures of the ratio of useful to useless documents.

If we put into the patron's hands eight documents, and six of them are useful to the patron, as in the top portion of figure 5.7, then we have a figure of 75 percent for precision. If we put eight documents into the patron's hands and only two of them are useful, then we have a 25 percent precision figure.

U U N U

N U U U

U = useful
N = not useful

$$6U/6U+2N = 6/8 = 3/4 = 75\% \text{ Precision}$$

or

N N U N

N U N N

U = useful
N = not useful

$$2U/2U+6N = 2/8 = 1/4 = 25\% \text{ Precision}$$

Fig. 5.7. Precision: Ratio of useful documents to total documents in hand.

If we know that of the 20 documents in the collection, 8 are useful and 6 of those useful documents are put into the patron's hands, then we have a 75 percent recall, as shown in the top portion of figure 5.8. If we put into the hands of the patron only two of those eight documents, then we have only a 25 percent recall figure.

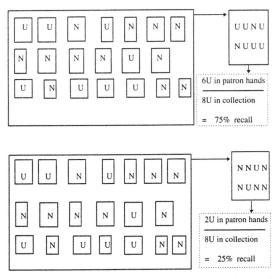

Fig. 5.8. Recall: ratio of relevant documents in hand to total relevant documents.

There is generally an inverse relationship between precision and recall. That is, if one casts a broad net to be sure one gets everything one wants (high recall), one is also likely to get a lot that is not useful (low precision). If, in contrast, one aims to have very little useless material (high precision), one risks missing useful material (low recall).

We must return to some of the difficulties with the concepts of precision and recall that diminish their utility as measurements of the representational capabilities of a system. To determine how many of the works in a patron's hands are useful is no great task. It may take some time for the patron to do sufficient analysis to make such a determination, but it is a relatively simple task. There are, of course, some circumstances under which the patron might not realize that a potentially useful work is so; or it might only be in retrospect, after some time, that the utility is recognized. In general, though, the variables are knowable and the process is simple: Count what is in hand, count how many are useful, calculate the ratio.

More troubling is the concept of recall, in terms of what is not known (or not easily knowable). How are we to know the total number of useful works in the collection? If we do not know the total of useful works, how can we calculate a ratio? If we know all the works that would be useful, why did we not put them into the patron's hands?

If we leave the patron out of the loop and simply count subject headings in hand and compare those with subject heading numbers known for the collection, then we can deliver a number. However, we have to ask if we have measured anything useful. Blair and Maron demonstrated the efficacy of a sophisticated statistical sampling and analysis technique for providing a well-educated guess about the total number of useful documents in a collection.[5] However, the system resources and the time commitments required of the patron to do this are prohibitive in most circumstances.

To distinguish only "useful" from "not useful" yields a binary system. This burdens the indexer with the task of being right on target for every user. In many instances, a user will say, "This one was pretty good; this one was only good for the pictures; this one was a waste of time; this one was great." In other words, user satisfaction is rarely a binary entity.

If the indexer wants to satisfy every user who might be happy to find the document, even for just one photograph or three pages or two minutes of an hour-long video, he or she must construct a representation with many elements. However, this is likely to put a lot of trash into the hands of some patrons. The patron searching for material for a paper on Jeffersonian concepts of democracy in developing countries would not be happy to have a work in hand tagged with "democracy" because there is one paragraph about the role of postsecondary education in a democracy.

We return to considering depth of indexing with some questions:

- Is there an ideal set of indexing terms for each document?

- Is there an optimal depth of indexing?

Yes, but there is a catch. If we accept the notion that a patron's requirements and decoding abilities determine the level of specificity of elements highlighted and the mode of representation, then we must qualify our answers. Yes, but these are not single entities. Rather, the ideal is likely to be different for each different use of the system.

Extensional depth or *exhaustivity of indexing* is frequently used synonymously with *breadth of indexing*. Each of these phrases speaks to the number of terms assigned to each document in a collection. We may define *breadth* as the total number of terms assigned to the whole collection divided by the number of different terms assigned within the collection.

In our collection of 20 documents, if we had a total of 100 terms applied to the collection, we could look at breadth in these ways:

100 terms in all applied/16 different terms used = breadth of 6.25

100 terms in all applied/27 different terms used = breadth of 3.7

100 terms in all applied/63 different terms used = breadth of 1.59

If we have 20 documents and 100 terms, we can assume that there is an average of 5 terms per document. If we have only 16 terms from which to choose those 5 for each document, our choices are limited. As we increase the number of available terms to 27 or 63, we increase our choices for describing each document.

In our preceding samples, we see that as our choices increase, the numerical representation of breadth decreases. We can think of this in terms of a given volume of liquid (say, one quart) in different containers. If the container has a large diameter (say, 6.25), the liquid will be shallow in the container. As the diameter decreases, the depth increases. Thus, a diameter of 3.7 yields a deeper body of liquid, and 1.59 yields a still deeper body. So, the lower the breadth number, the greater the breadth.

Intensional depth refers to the semantic detail available from the indexing vocabulary. We can define this as the total number of term assignments made in the collection divided by the total number of documents. In the example of differences in breadth, we said we had 20 documents and 100 terms, which yielded an average (intensional depth) of 5. If we assume the same collection of 20 documents, we can see that the higher the resulting value, the greater the intensional depth:

- 100 terms assigned/20 documents = 5
- 525 terms assigned/20 documents = 26.25
- 917 terms assigned/20 documents = 45.85

Specificity is a term addressing two closely related concepts:

- Ability of the indexing language to describe documents precisely
- Actual level of the documents represented

A set of relationships typically holds between precision and recall on the one hand, and exhaustivity (breadth) and specificity on the other. These relationships can be summarized as in table 5.1 on page 70.

This suggests that the more broad terms we apply to each document (greater exhaustivity), the more likely the patron is to get desirable materials (high recall), but at the cost of having more undesirable material through which to sift (low precision). The broad terms do not address the degree to which any particular document is "about" the term. Similarly, if we apply very specific terms to each document, we may well hide from the patron works that are closely related but described a little bit differently.

Table 5.1
Precision/Recall Relationships

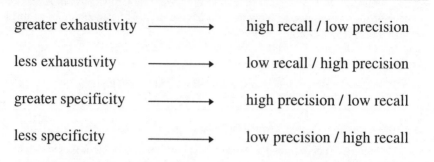

greater exhaustivity ——————→ high recall / low precision

less exhaustivity ——————→ low recall / high precision

greater specificity ——————→ high precision / low recall

less specificity ——————→ low precision / high recall

Extensional depth (exhaustivity) is generally imposed by the bibliographic agency posited in the general model in figure 4.2. That is, the agency producing the representations of the documents sets the number of descriptive terms to be used. There is a counter model that does not impose any particular level of exhaustivity. Maron, Cooper, and Robertson posit a model that includes the patron in the representation.[6] Although the goal of putting into the hands of the patron all the documents that the patron would find useful, and only those documents, is not unique, the underlying assumption of the model represents a significant shift. Representation actively includes the user.

The basic model can be summarized as follows. For any given descriptive term and any single patron, we can ask, "If the patron were to use this term to describe the information requirement, would he or she be happy to find this document?" If the answer is yes, then apply the term as a descriptor; if it is no, then do not. We can then extend the question to cover all patrons (or all likely patrons), either by asking the same question over and over with each patron in mind, or by keeping track of how many patrons are satisfied over time. The system, in effect, knows: "Of those who used this term in their search, 83 percent were happy with document A, 47 percent with document B, and 91 percent with document C."

The system could set a cut-off point, for example: "Any document rated over 90 percent will be shown to the patron." However, the system does not know how much material the user needs, or the purpose (if one is writing a critique of a field, the works not liked by others could be of great interest), or the time and interest level available. The solution is simply to make available the ranking of the collection. Thus, if a patron needs "just any good work or two on X," he or she need only look to works in the top 5 or 10 percent. The patron writing a dissertation could check down to the 30 percent level or even less. The patron needing to write a brief report, but finding the items in the top 10 percent unavailable, could examine items in the 80 percent range.

There are numerous variations of the ranking model, but a key element in them is the concern for the user in the construction of (or, at least, control over) the representation. This enables a closer fit between the system and the user in terms of the elements selected for highlighting, as well as the coding system.

Earlier we asked the questions:

- Which elements should be extracted?

- How many elements should be extracted?

- What form should the descriptors have?

Our definition of *representation* suggests these answers:

- Extract whichever elements are useful to the patron

- Extract however many elements are necessary for the patron

- Employ whatever form is consistent with patron abilities and requirements

We have begun to explore the concepts underlying the implementation of such answers. Depth and breadth of representation, together with precision and recall, are attempts to model the attributes of the collection that would enable a system to be constructed. The premises are flawed, however, if they do not include both the patron and the documents.

Our subsequent explorations will weave together additional theoretical constructs and case studies to illuminate the user-collection relationship. Though we will examine means of refining system abilities to describe patron knowledge states and knowledge states represented by documents, we do not advocate a single, one-size-fits-all system. Rather, we will be suggesting the nature and components of a vital organization capable of responding appropriately to varying conditions and requirements.

Notes

1. This chapter is largely derived from the work of David Blair on modeling indeterminacy, or the likelihood of disjunction between a user's needs and abilities on the one hand and an indexer's representations on the other.

2. W. S. Cooper, "Is Interindexer Consistency a Deep Hobgoblin?" *American Documentation* 20, no. 3 (July 1969): 100-110.

3. Patrick Wilson, "The Catalog as Access Mechanism: Background and Concepts," *Library Resources and Technical Services* (January 1983): 5-17.

4. Brian O'Connor, "Browsing: A Framework for Seeking Functional Information," *Knowledge: Creation, Diffusion, Utilization* 15, no. 2 (1993): 211-32. Of particular interest for this discussion is page 211, which lists studies of the use of standard bibliographic tools by researchers in the hard sciences, the social sciences, and the humanities. Each of the studies shows that little or no use is made of these tools in the creative phase of research.

5. David C. Blair and M. E. Maron, "An Evaluation of Retrieval Effectiveness for a Full-Text Document-Retrieval System," *Communications of the ACM* 28, no. 3 (1985): 289-99. The abstract of the article states: "An evaluation of a large, operational full-text document-retrieval system . . . shows the system to be retrieving less than 20 percent of the documents relevant to a particular search."

6. M. E. Maron, W. S. Cooper, and S. E. Robertson, "Probability of Relevance: A Unification of Two Competing Models for Document Retrieval," *Information Technology: Research and Development* 1, no. 1 (1982): 1-21. The introduction to the article and sections 2.2 (meaning of relevance) and 2.3 (enter probability of relevance) are of special interest to this portion of our explorations. The concept of user-centeredness or user inclusion can also be seen just by skimming titles in the recent literature. For example, these articles appeared in 1994:

- H. W. Bruce, "A Cognitive View of the Situational Dynamism of User-Centered Relevance Estimation," *Journal of the American Society for Information Science* 45, no. 3 (1994): 142-48.

- D. A. Michel, "What Is Used During Cognitive Processing in Information Retrieval and Library Searching? Eleven Sources of Search Information," *Journal of the American Society for Information Science* 45, no. 7 (1994): 142-48.

- J. W. Janes, "Other People's Judgments: A Comparison of Users' and Others' Judgments of Document Relevance, Topicality, and Utility," *Journal of the American Society for Information Science* 45, no. 3 (1994): 160-71.

- C. L. Barry, "User-Defined Relevance Criteria: An Exploratory Study," *Journal of the American Society for Information Science* 45, no. 3 (1994): 149-59.

- T. K. Park, "Toward a Theory of User-Based Relevance: A Call for a New Paradigm of Inquiry," *Journal of the American Society for Information Science* 45, no. 3 (1994): 135-41.

- R. C. T. Morris, "Toward a User-Centered Information Service," *Journal of the American Society for Information Science* 45, no. 1 (1994): 20-30.

- C. Watters and M. A. Shepherd, "Shifting the Information Paradigm from Data-Centered to User-Centered," *Information Processing and Management* 30, no. 4 (1994): 455-72.

Chapter 6
Responses to Subject Indeterminacy

Resolving search failures resulting from incompatibilities between user representations and document collection representation systems is generally accomplished in one of two ways, commonly termed *reference* and *browsing*. If the patron can give voice to a topic or set of topics that would fill the information gap, then adjustment of patron and system representation conventions can be made with the intervention of a reference librarian or other system intermediary.

Search failures in instances when the information need can be articulated suggest that:

- Different terminologies are being used for the same concept

- The patron is unsure of the level of specificity required

- The patron is unsure of knowledge structures in areas that might be helpful

- The patron has a vague awareness of the problem, but cannot articulate it well

In such cases, the system can provide assistance in translating and refining the search terms. The assumption is that the patron and the system have represented the appropriate parts of the object/event space in similar ways. All that is required is adjustment of the conventions for coding and decoding. System assistance may be in the form of:

- a reference librarian

- a database search intermediary

- on-line help screens

- transparent systems of adjustment (e.g., system searches for "Twain" and for "Clemens" even if the patron only types in "Twain")

- some form of user-inclusive (e.g., weighted query) interface

- combinations and expansions of these approaches

More difficult and less amenable to simple translation efforts are searches that are "functional."[1] Such searches do not have an articulated target concept or topic. They are based on finding *any* information that fulfills a functional need. Because there is no expressed topic, there is no issue of adjusting representations of the topic.

A powerful response to failures of this sort is to ignore the system's representation conventions entirely. A patron assumes that any part of the collection is just as likely as any other part to yield useful results. Idiosyncratic methods of sampling and evaluating are substituted for topic representation.

Reference librarians and browsing are the focal points for our considerations of responses to subject indeterminacy. Reference work here is considered in terms of translation and adjustment. Browsing by scholars is our focus for personal approaches to sampling document collections. Browsing occupies considerable space in our explorations because it is so important, yet is seldom articulated as a search strategy.

Patrons and Intermediaries: Partners in the Search Process

If a patron had all the time in the world, and the ability to conduct a search, there would be little need for intermediaries such as reference librarians or database searchers. As this is rarely the case, such intermediaries are often useful partners in the search process. Representation abilities account, in large part, for the utility of intermediaries.

Intermediaries function, in general, to reconcile patron representation abilities with the collection. Translation and ad hoc use of "chunking" are the primary representation capabilities of intermediaries. Intermediary activity can be modeled as in figure 6.1.

The intermediary, through observation and conversation, establishes an attribute palette[2] of the patron. At the same time, the patron establishes an attribute palette of the intermediary's abilities. Conversation, in its broadest sense, establishes:

- common ground or a joint attribute palette[3]

- the nature of the patron's question state

- a jointly constructed request attribute palette

The request attribute palette is used to establish some subset of candidate documents. This may be accomplished by inserting the request into the formal retrieval apparatus, or it may be accomplished by the intermediary making use of personal knowledge that represents document contents in a different manner. We might say that the intermediary uses the jointly constructed request to find and interrogate documents with some overlap with the patron's information need. The patron (perhaps with assistance) determines the sufficiency and significance of the overlap. The degree of sufficiency and overlap help determine whether additional searching is required and, if so, where it should be done.

Representation of the patron's question state is enhanced by the intermediary's:

- knowledge of representation conventions within the collection

- elicitation of potentially relevant concepts from the patron

- iterative evaluation with the patron of sample documents

- ability to refine the request attribute palette according to evaluations

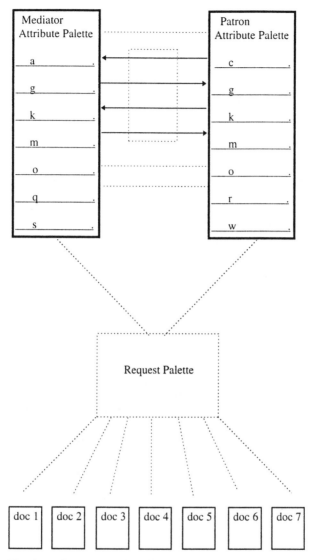

Fig. 6.1. Joint construction of request by patron and intermediary.

Representation of the documents is enhanced by the intermediary's:

- subtle understanding of formal representation conventions
- ability to translate user terms to system terms
- understanding of what may exist at different levels of specificity
- knowledge of document structures
- knowledge of content clusters across documents
- critical evaluation abilities

In its simplest implementation, this model requires little understanding of user attributes by the intermediary or intermediary attributes by the user. Only the words used by the patron to express an information requirement are considered. A topic that would satisfy the patron has been expressed, but it is in terms different from those used for representations of the collection. The intermediary merely finds a synonym, or the proper level of specificity, or the proper form of expression. The model's true virtue lies in its ability to use the formal representation system as a framework to support translation, linkages across levels of specificity, and linkages between segments of formal clusters of documents. All this is accomplished as an intermediary representation in the service of aligning a patron's coding with that of the system and bringing need and document together.

Browsing

Creative scholarly work requires functional access.[4] There is a perception by researchers in a variety of fields that serendipity, luck, browsing, or some such process standing outside the formal bibliographical apparatus has made a significant contribution to their work. Profiles of scholars in the sciences, social sciences, and humanities indicate that researchers make little use of the established access mechanisms for finding documents. The standard formal systems for representing documents often do not present the researcher with adequate means for discovering catalytic works. Browsing is a means for accomplishing such discovery.

Browsing leaves the decision of what is to be represented up to the patron. It leaves depth of penetration into the collection and into each individual document up to the patron. The tradeoff in this method is the requirement for more patron resources of time and effort. Clearly, for many patrons browsing is not an option. Yet for those engaged in the creation of new knowledge, as well as those who have been frustrated in any form of search, browsing may be the best method of searching.

We can see browsing as a form of indexing and abstracting. Representation of the collection and of individual documents is still accomplished—except the *patron* is now the agent of representation. Pointing to parts of the collection is accomplished in some random fashion. Selection of attributes takes place ad hoc rather than a priori. In the standard bibliographic apparatus, the agency sets the rules for representation of documents, representation of questions, and the method of comparing the two; in browsing, the patron:

- is in control of location and depth of engagement with the collection
- formulates the rules for highlighting
- constructs the coding system
- determines the acceptability of tradeoffs
- assumes responsibility

In a very real sense, the browser has chosen our earlier proposition that one could examine the whole collection until what was sought was found. The constraints of time are loosened by sampling methods rather than by dependence on the pointing and summarizing abilities of others.

Browsing as Searching Without a Topic

Browsing consists of a wide spectrum of idiosyncratic processes for searching, sampling, and evaluating documents when significant attributes of a target or goal are not fully articulated or evident. Serendipity is, here, not dumb luck, but rather the willingness of the scholar to "search in a literature not obviously relevant," to acknowledge the possible value of an unlikely item, to make many connections, and to make evaluations.

We need to be aware of a critical distinction that has roots in the agricultural etymology of *browsing*. The *Oxford English Dictionary*[5] notes that *browse* means:

> to feed on the leaves and shoots of trees and shrubs; to crop the shoots or tender parts . . . (sometimes carelessly used for "graze," but properly implying the cropping of scanty vegetation).

The entry on grazing adds:

> To feed on growing grass and other herbage. . . . To put [cattle] to feed on pasture; also to tend while feeding.

When an animal is browsing, it is hunting for sustenance; it must find and evaluate the food. When an animal is grazing, it is simply eating in an area where supply and evaluation are not issues. Browsing is deliberate searching. So, too, for the scholar browsing is serious work; it is a deliberate search for new connections or support for those new connections. Browsing is not idle, purposeless, or undirected, though it may not have a clearly defined target topic.

We might do better to use *grazing* for many of the activities in a library or database that are often termed browsing. When librarians put related works near one another on the shelves, they are typically said to be supporting browsing. Yet, by determining which connections establish relatedness, they are supplying the pasture and tending to the user; they are supporting grazing.

When someone is searching, he or she must be searching for *something*. However, that something need not be well conceptualized or clearly articulated. *Something* can be the function of filling in a knowledge gap, without the scholar being able to specify a topic that would fill the gap. A scholar may well set out, rather like a detective, knowing a problem area but having little or no preconceived topical description. For a scholar's query to be well conceptualized, it may, indeed, be necessary that it *not* be tagged, precisely so that it will not be hampered by the inappropriate satisfaction derived from an "illusion of knowledge."[6]

We noted earlier that one still cannot walk up to a reference librarian and ask to be shown the new knowledge documents. If it can be given a subject heading and pointed to, it is already known, so it is not available to be made new. Similarly, we ought not to expect a scholar to be able to give a topical description to a knowledge gap. This in no way implies a lack of deliberateness.

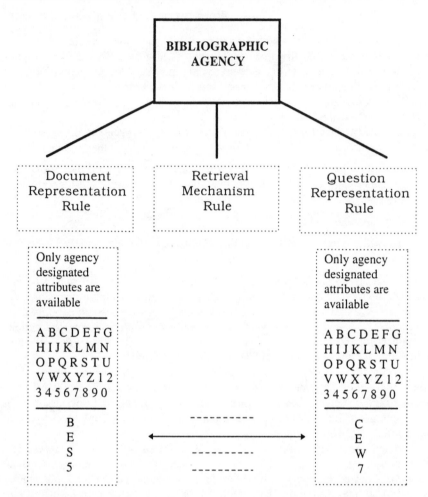

Fig. 6.2. System determines which document attributes and searcher attributes are to be considered for retrieval.

As discussed in chapter 4, the bibliographical apparatus determines which subset of the attributes of each document is to be made available (see fig. 6.2). Likewise, it establishes which subset of attributes of the searcher is useable in a search. The attributes of the document that are typically represented include descriptive tags, such as author, title, date, and publisher, as well as subject descriptors for topics determined by the system to be addressed by the work. The attributes of the scholar that are typically allowed are descriptive rather than functional; for example, simple topic descriptions of the question, languages of acceptable documents, dates, and publishers.

It may be that there is a fundamental disjunction between the purposes of the formal bibliographical apparatus and the requirements of the scholar. Reduction of ambiguity is a compelling reason for much of the descriptive cataloging and the subject analysis that are provided as access mechanisms. Yet, thriving on ambiguity is recognized as a primary quality of creative activity.

Browsing Activities

Browsing provides the scholar with the means to rectify the situation of no overlap between the query concept (whether articulated or vague or not posited at all) and the terms applied by the bibliographical agency. Different sampling strategies are engaged depending on the reason for the lack of overlap.

The various strategies for browsing can each be identified with one of the sorts of internal functional representation of an anomalous state of knowledge that a scholar might bring to a collection. Each of these is distinct from the topical retrieval for which the typical bibliographical apparatus is designed. The type of anomalous state of knowledge any scholar brings to a collection will determine which sampling and evaluation strategies are put into play; yet there are significant commonalities.

Browsing approaches the difficulties posed by subject indeterminacy by removing constraints on the content and size of attribute lists for both the searcher and the document. The scholar may engage any attribute or set of attributes, no matter how unrelated it might seem to any particular topic. Hobby interests, title of an undergraduate course, cognitive style, political leanings, color preferences, and numerous other self-descriptors, ranging from the seemingly trivial to the seemingly substantial, may be engaged in an ad hoc way as a search goes on.

The functional requirements stimulating the search will guide the choice of starting point, sampling point, and evaluation criteria. Similarly, the studiousness of the searcher will determine the sampling size, search evaluation, and number of iterations of the process. The physical nature of the collection (that is, whether it is a collection of hard-copy documents, a full-text database, or database of representations) will likely affect the manner in which glimpses are made and the locations in which they are made.

Each of four sorts of browsing activity is described in terms of:

- point in the collection at which browsing starts

- sampling size

- which attributes of the document are considered

- which attributes of the scholar are engaged

- sort of comparison between document and scholar attributes

The four sorts of activity that we consider to constitute browsing are regions on a spectrum of activity, rather than distinct activities. They share the attributes previously listed and they all assume that the searcher does the representation and the evaluation of documents. The four sorts of activity are:

1. Expansion
2. Segmenting and ranking (vague awareness)
3. Monitoring the information environment
4. Catalyzing new knowledge (shaking up the knowledge store)

Expansion. Expansion could be termed a near-known-topic search. In a sense, it is the boundary case between grazing and browsing. The arrangement of documents on a shelf or in a file by closeness of topics is similar to putting an animal in a pasture. If a suitable document is found, documents with a similarity to some of its attributes will be nearby. So long as the attribute on which shelf position was determined is the attribute sought by the scholar, expansion to either side may yield useful results.

Such a browsing activity begins as a targeted search. However, to the degree that nearby topics were not originally considered or articulated, their subsequent engagement yields a functional search. The boundary between the topical and the functional—between grazing and browsing—is porous.

The sampling location is specified by the location of a known item or known class. The size of the sample is limited only by studiousness. There exists a high overlap between the query attribute list and the document attribute list. Moving away from the original target document may present data or attributes or ways of characterizing attributes that had previously been overlooked; thus, it is not necessarily the case that movement from the known item will result in less overlap of document and query, so much as it may result in a modification of the query.

Vague Awareness. Vague-awareness searches are conducted when the searcher is aware of a problem or a lack but is not able to state concisely and exactly what it is, though a useful document would be recognized if glimpsed. The searcher makes use of the formal bibliographic apparatus to make a first-order partitioning of the collection by ranked probabilities of utility. The primary concept is to maximize the amount of useful data one takes in for analysis.

Suppose you notice frequent use of similar metaphors in news reports about some illness and you begin to wonder about:

- something like the mythology of illness

- or social consequences of the representation of disease

- or the feminine "virtue" of consumption and how that relates to AIDS funding

- or "something like that" dealing with representation and illness

That is, you have a curiosity about all the ways in which disease is seen as something beyond a mere assault of some infectious agent or a biological process gone awry.

You might look to the Library of Congress Subject Headings list for something like Representation of Disease, but find that there is no such heading. You might try a keyword search using "disease" and "representation," which would yield a work such as *Disease and Representation: Images of Illness from Madness to AIDS*. References in this work might prove interesting, though the Library of Congress Subject Headings applied to the work probably would not.

The Library of Congress Subject Headings used to represent this book are:

- Mental illness—History

- Diseases in art

- Disease—Psychology

- Medicine in art

- Sick role

The two that mention art might prove useful, though there would likely be many works listed under these headings with little relevance to your search.

You might recall that Susan Sontag had written something about illness and metaphor. An author search would turn up *Illness as Metaphor* (New York: Farrar, Straus & Giroux, 1978) and *AIDS and Its Metaphors* (New York: Farrar, Straus & Giroux, 1989). These also might have some interesting references. If you were to happen upon a work by Lakeoff, you might find insights about individual and social representation. However, again there is no obvious connection between societal representation of disease and the subject headings such as Categorization (Psychology), Cognition, and Thought and Thinking under which much of Lakoff's work is grouped. Therefore, it is unlikely that you would come across his works just by means of a subject search.

You might not immediately think of looking under Women in Art or in the N (Fine Arts) section of the collection, yet here you would come across a work with a title not obviously relevant *(Idols of Perversity)* but a chapter entitled "The Cult of Invalidism." This chapter examines the role of painting in "exploit[ing] and romanticiz[ing] the notion of woman as a permanent, a necessary, even a 'natural' invalid. It was an image which in the second half of the nineteenth century came to control and not infrequently destroy the lives of countless European and American women." [7] This and the associated references might be of considerable interest to you.

Again, though it might be possible to characterize your knowledge gap by giving examples of possible areas or items of interest, there is no single or small set of topical descriptors. In such a search there is no specific sampling location, other than the broad segmenting of the collection into zones likely and less likely to prove fruitful *(ranking)*. Also, there is no particular sample size, though the size is likely to be small, so as to maximize the number of glimpses per time unit. There is a relaxed specification for the threshold of overlap of query attributes and document attributes.

Monitoring the Information Environment. Monitoring the information environment rests on an assumption by the individual scholar that he or she does not know everything, even within an individual discipline. No clearly articulated query can be made; rather, sampling methods that keep the scholar aware of new developments are instituted. This may mean skimming tables of contents, scanning shelves in particular portions of a collection for new titles, or even chatting with colleagues.

Location and size of sample are preset based on the satisfactory level of overlap of attribute lists in previous experience. That is, the scholar chooses a region with high variability in attribute values. This might be the new acquisitions section or new nonfiction display. It may also be a sampling mechanism (or set of mechanisms) with a constrained set of attributes (appropriate language, reading ability, fields cognate with interests of the searcher).

One simple implementation of this approach is in common use now: the recent acquisitions collection or new book section. Herein a small number of documents, each of which is likely to be recent, is present, sometimes in classified order and sometimes in random order. Such a subset collection usually contains documents from fields across the breadth of the whole collection. Any document that seems interesting will likely contain references and descriptors leading back into the whole collection. Time is condensed and novelty is likely to be high.

Catalyzing New Knowledge. Catalyzing new knowledge, or *creativity*, may be called as the ability to make combinations of dichotomous or previously unrelated concepts and then evaluate the combination for a possible fit or for a more accommodating model. Browsing enables the combination of user-selected characteristics of the searcher with a user-selected set of characteristics of a document and evaluation of the utility of the combination.

Because the intent is to generate a new combination, there is no way to segment the collection. Short of engaging each and every document, a random sampling is made on the assumption that any location is just as likely as any other to yield fruitful results.

This approach to browsing assumes an extremely relaxed threshold of congruence between scholar attributes and document attributes. There is no prespecification (prediction) of useful class or individual entity attributes that are likely to be useful (except, perhaps, for the negative specification of "NOT the documents or class[es] with which I am already familiar"). Also, there is no specification of search query attributes, except for the limiting case of "I know I don't know what I need to know, so I will entertain any combination of attributes." That is, neither the sampling location nor the sampling size nor the degree of congruence of attribute lists is specified.

Willful violation of the concept of least effort is at the heart of such searching. A searcher gives up the reduction of search time and search space provided by the formal apparatus in turn for freedom to represent as required. Informal discussions with faculty members working in two large research libraries yielded several variations of one strategy that suggests both the idiosyncratic nature of browsing and the expectation of greater effort:

1.   Park your car.

2.   Write down the license number of a nearby car.

3.   Enter collection where the call numbers match the license plate number.

4.   Do some sampling.

5.   Expect that most of the time your search will yield little or nothing.

6.   Hope that the search just might yield the spark to ignite a new idea.

Components of Browsing Activity

Having looked at four sorts of browsing activity, we can now examine the primary components of each of those activities. In a sense, these are the subgoals that were achieved by the steps or attributes discussed earlier. We may give the subgoals or components useful labels:

1.   Make glimpses.

2.   Connect attributes.

3.   Evaluate connection.

4.   Evaluate search.

Make Glimpses. The first phase in the process of discovering a "difference that makes a difference" is the examination of document attributes. To evaluate a document's potential for resolving an anomalous state of knowledge, a searcher must read (*engage* may be a better term for documents in various media) all the coding, some subset of the coding, or some comprehensible representation of that coding. Morse proposed that maximizing the likelihood of discovery depends on maximizing the number of glimpses per time unit.[8] Each glimpse is the inputting of one document attribute to the searcher's connection-making system.

Selection of a starting point within a collection or identification of a sector to be searched amounts to a global glimpse of the megadocument that constitutes the collection. The likely importance of the selection and the manner in which the selection is made both depend on the type of question initiating the response. If the searcher has a vague idea of what would be a useful document, it may be useful to select portions of the collection that have some connection to the concept. If the searcher is seeking "to shake up the knowledge store"[9] in an effort to generate or sustain creative activity, a random starting point will likely be engaged (though not entirely random, as the portion of the collection with which the searcher is familiar will probably be left out of the search).

Examination of attributes of individual documents is glimpsing at the local level. A searcher seeks to minimize the time between useful glimpses without inhibiting the ability to evaluate the attribute made evident by any individual glimpse. The individual glimpse is the instrument that enables the searcher to create the appropriate representation system. If representation is taken to be the set of rules by which certain elements of a document are selected or highlighted, then the browsing searcher can be seen as the rule maker. As such, the searcher can vary the rules as input (or lack of input) warrants. The value of an attribute and even the sort of attribute are determined ad hoc by the scholar interacting with the collection.

Control over depth of penetration into a collection was identified in the Intrex study as a primary attribute of browsing. The collection of documents is, in effect, a stream of data only incidentally segmented into books, videos, or database records. A searcher may start at any point on the virtual stream of documents and move at will to other points, making glimpses of large physical and conceptual chunks of the data within the collection (for example, classification segments, series, or individual whole documents). At any point along the stream, the user may penetrate the collection to greater and greater depth—chapter, verse, sentence, or phrase, for example, as illustrated in figure 6.3. Any datum at a particular depth can be related to any other datum at any other depth at the same point on the stream or any depth at any other point on the stream.

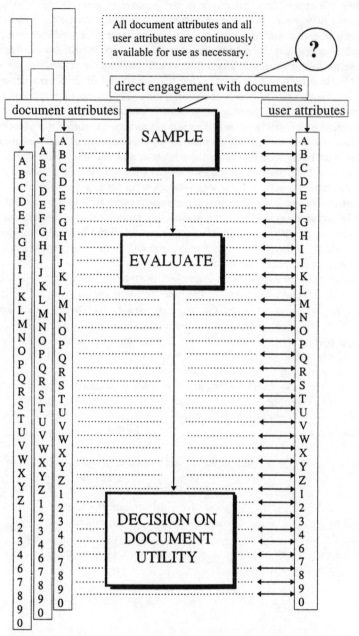

Fig. 6.3. In browsing, the user is responsible for representation.

Such control enables the searcher to represent the document at any useful level of specificity and at any point within the document. Because the glimpses input data directly from the document, there is no issue of translation or differing terms for the same concept, as happens when an external representation of the document is made.

There is still no certainty that the searcher will discover a useful concept, even if a particular work in hand addresses it. The sample size or number of document data items considered at each glimpse may be the wrong size to catch or emphasize the contents that address the issue; the searcher may not have the vocabulary or expertise to decode the text appropriately; or, if new knowledge is being sought, a relevant concept may just not be recognizable.

Connect Attributes. Central to creative activity is *gullibility,*[10] which may be taken as a "willingness to catch similarities" or the holding of two or more seemingly antithetical propositions. This requires that searchers "know themselves"; that is, have available the full array of appropriate attributes (and their current values) of their internal representations. The type of search will determine which attributes are likely to be of value. If there is a vague awareness of the knowledge gap driving the search, then titles and subtitles within a limited set of subject areas might be appropriate. If the search is driven by a desire to generate new knowledge, then it may be impossible to predict what attribute or attribute value is likely to be meaningful.

A searcher may look to document attributes of any sort and any size at any level of specificity. Single words, entire chapters (or analogs in other media), style, level of presumed expertise, type of graphics, authorial stance, color of binding, and location in a collection are but a few of the physical attributes and conceptual attributes that might be considered by a searcher.

A document or set of documents likely to comprise an answer would share some significant set of attributes with the description of the searcher. Search query attributes (which in browsing may range from a limited set of one or a few qualities to an unspecified and volatile set, in the sense that those brought into play at any particular point may vary) and document attributes are compared through some sampling mechanism.

Three sorts of connections between document attributes and searcher attributes are possible:

1. A particular document attribute may be paired with a particular searcher attribute for evaluation as a valid proposition.

2. A document attribute may link or act as a catalyst for linking two attributes of the searcher's internal representation of the problem.

3. An internal representation attribute may link or serve as a catalyst for linking two document attributes.

Achieving some threshold degree of overlap between document attributes and searcher attributes yields a candidate document for filling the knowledge gap. Of course, determination of what constitutes significant overlap remains with the searcher. One attribute might be sufficient, or some threshold percentage might be required. Then, either the general characteristics of the class or the document attributes that are not congruent with the query attributes can be used to fill in the scholar's knowledge gap or to refine the search process.

Evaluate Connection. Just as browsing transfers the representation of both documents and queries to the searcher, so too it transfers the responsibility for evaluation of documents. For the bibliographical apparatus, evaluation is typically a statement of whether there is a match or a significant overlap of topic descriptors for questions and topic descriptors for documents. This reduces the burden of analysis for the searcher, yet presents the difficulties and failures of subject indeterminacy.

Conversation between the hemispheres of the human information processing paradigms brings together the pattern-recognition capabilities of the "right" and the logico-symbolic capabilities of the "left." In the idiosyncratic search, the combinations of attributes generated from glimpsed data are subjected to the testing and scrutiny of the searcher's evaluative abilities, as illustrated in figure 6.4. To paraphrase Pauling: "The way to come up with good ideas is to generate a lot of connections and simply throw out the bad ones."[11]

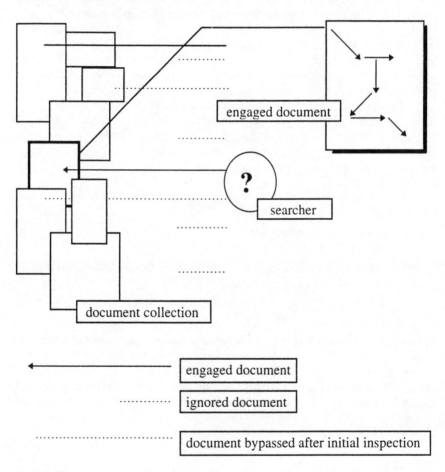

Fig. 6.4. The user controls the point of entry and level of specificity.

Of course, the means for simply throwing out the bad are not entirely self-evident, and they may well bear little resemblance to the formal methodologies of any relevant discipline (though it is not likely that the evaluations will be made with total disregard for such methods). The momentary validity of a linkage or proposition will rest on a pattern ("right" hemisphere evaluation) rather than logical analysis. A linkage that does not in itself prove valid may yet show the way to another that does.

The evaluative conversation, like gullibility, presupposes considerable studiousness in at least two senses. First, there has been time allocated to immersion in a topic or set of topics. Such immersion undergirds the recognition of patterns and the facility with methodology normally associated with expertise. Second, the time and ability applied within the individual search are likely to be considerable, though, of course, the possibility of finding a useful item early in a search exists.

Evaluate Search. Linked closely to the connection evaluation is evaluation of the search as a whole. The outcome of the connection evaluation is likely to be one of these:

- This is a satisfactory connection

- This is not a satisfactory connection

- No decision can be made

If the connection is judged to be satisfactory (which need not mean that it will hold up to further scrutiny, but only that it seems worth pursuing), then the search may be considered complete. It may be that browsing will continue, but this might be considered a second search if the scholar is looking for yet other new connections; or it may be that the nature of the search changes as the scholar looks for supportive materials.

If a connection is judged unsatisfactory, then a decision must be made about the search as a whole. Are there sufficient resources (time, enthusiasm, money) to continue searching at this time? If the search is to be continued, a decision has to be made at the local level: should sampling continue at the same level or with the same attribute, or should the sample location change?

The absence of a clearly articulated target suggests that there may be no means of determining when a search is finished. Discovery of a useful document may signal the end of the search, or it may suggest a line of continued search. Exhaustion of resources may bring a halt to the current search process, but need not be considered a failed search. At the least, the portions of the collection examined this time need not be considered the next time (unless, of course, a discovery in a subsequent search triggers a connection with a previously examined document).

Discussion. The personal nature of searching in "literature not obviously relevant"[12] does not necessarily render the bibliographical apparatus useless. Even if the searcher is the primary agent of representation, system resources can enable more rapid presentation of attributes, as well as more rapid and more informed evaluation of connections. Keyword searching, rapid scanning of long lists of hits, and "Internet surfing" from one library to another (within seconds) already speak to the capability of system resources to shrink the time required to examine document attributes.

Mechanisms of abstract construction also enable a system to facilitate idiosyncratic browsing activity. An abstract enables a searcher to make a decision while expending less effort than would be required to engage the whole document. The document collection can be taken as one large document; so far as the scholar is concerned, the boundaries imposed by book covers or database files are of little consequence, as long as useful information is found.

There will likely be varying degrees of articulation of the knowledge gap. Optimal searching for some levels of articulation will require segmenting the collection and assigning probabilities of likely utility. Our question in this circumstance asks, "How does the scholar 'crop the scanty vegetation' in order to bring to light 'undiscovered public knowledge'?"[13] We then have to decide if we can construct tools to facilitate scanning, penetrating, and evaluating. Are there times when simply stepping aside entirely is the best method of facilitating representation? Can we make evident to scholars the fact that searching depends on representation and that there are concrete elements to the activity that could be optimized?

Responses to Indeterminacy

Intermediaries and browsing activities serve the searcher by overcoming differences in representation systems. Intermediaries help to translate between coding systems and, at times, help to clarify patron concepts. They may also have "chunking" abilities that make connections not evident in the primary apparatus.[14] This may enable them to respond to questions that require information from deep portions of a document. They might be able to say:

- I remember a physics book with a little bit on Homer and the wine dark sea

- I was just reading a novel that discusses film lighting and politics

- There was a little article in last week's paper about El Niño and the weather

- There was a documentary on PBS just last night that had two minutes on this topic

The general model for the manner in which intermediary systems work is presented in figures 6.5 and 6.6, which are modifications of the models presented in chapter 5. Browsing steps outside the sytem; thus it avoids the system's deficiencies. However, it requires considerably more effort on the part of the searcher. It is, therefore, not an activity to be taken lightly. Figure 6.7 on page 90 further modifies the model of browsing found in chapter 5.

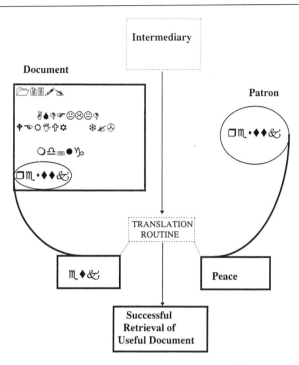

Fig. 6.5. An intermediary translates between differing representation systems.

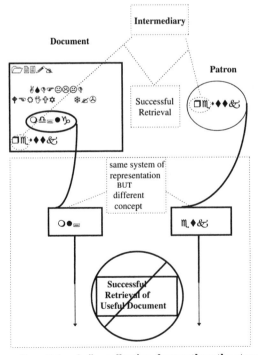

Fig. 6.6. An intermediary "chunks" a collection deeper than the standard apparatus.

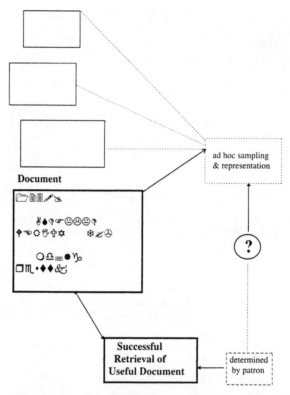

Fig. 6.7. Successful search without use of formal system, but at greater cost.

Intermediaries and browsing are powerful tools for the "discovery of the valuable in the mass of mostly worthless and uninteresting" documents.[15] Browsing activity offers us a probe. It is valued by scholars precisely because it operates outside the bounds of the formal access system. Therefore, it provides us a window through which to view expanded concepts of representation.

Notes

1.   Patrick Wilson, *Public Knowledge, Private Ignorance: Toward a Library and Information Policy* (Westport, Conn.: Greenwood Press, 1977). The concept of a functional approach is discussed, in particular, on page 120. The ramifications of this concept for the practice of bibliography are considered in Wilson's chapter entitled "Pragmatic Bibliography," in Howard D. White, Marcia Bates, and Patrick Wilson, in *For Information Specialists: Interpretations of Reference and Bibliographic Work* (Norwood, N.J.: Ablex, 1992), on pages 239-46.

2.   The term *attribute palette* was coined by Mary O'Connor during a discussion with the author about the Hayes article, "Measurement of Information," *Information Processing and Management* 29, no. 1 (1993): 1-11.

3. Brian O'Connor, "Browsing: A Framework for Seeking Functional Information," *Knowledge: Creation, Diffusion, Utilization* 15, no. 2 (1993): 211-32. See also Shan-Ju Chang and Ronald Rice, "Browsing: A Multidimensional Framework," *Annual Review of Information Science and Technology (ARIST)* 28 (1993): 231-76. This chapter examines the state of concepts and issues revolving around browsing.

4. J. F. Farrow, "A Cognitive Process Model of Document Indexing," *Journal of Documentation* 47, no. 2 (1991): 149-66. See also Brian O'Connor, "Fostering Creativity: Enhancing the Browsing Environment," *International Journal of Information Managment* 8 (19): 203-10.

5. J. A. Simpson and E. S. C. Weiner, eds., *Oxford English Dictionary* (Oxford: Clarendon, 1989).

6. S. Weisburd, "The Spark: Personal Testimonies of Creativity," *Science News* 132, no. 19 (1987): 299.

7. Bram Dijkstra, *Idols of Perversity: Fantasies of Feminine Evil in Fin-de-Siecle Culture* (New York: Oxford University Press, 1986).

8. Philip M. Morse, "Browsing and Search Theory," in *Toward a Theory of Librarianship: Papers in Honor of Jesse Hauk Shera*, edited by C. H. Rawsi (Metuchen, N.J.: Scarecrow Press, 1973), 246-61.

9. C. F. J. Overhage and R. J. Harman, eds., *Intrex: Report of a Planning Conference on Information Transfer Experiments* (Cambridge, Mass.: MIT, 1965).

10. J. P. Guilford, "Varieties of Divergent Thinking," *Journal of Creative Behavior* 18, no. 1 (1985): 1-10.

11. Weisburd, "The Spark," 299.

12. Overhage and Harman, *Intrex.*

13. Donald R. Swanson, "Undiscovered Public Knowledge," *Library Quarterly* 56, no. 2 (1986): 103-18.

14. Howard D. White, Marcia Bates, and Patrick Wilson, *For Information Specialists: Interpretations of Reference and Bibliographic Work* (Norwood, N.J.: Ablex, 1992).

15. Patrick Wilson, *Two Kinds of Power: An Essay on Bibliographic Control* (Berkeley: University of California Press, 1968).

Chapter 7

Enabling User Participation in Representation

One might well ask if there is any value to having indexing and abstracting systems. We have just spent considerable time discussing significant shortcomings of formal document representation systems. We have discussed reference intermediaries and browsing as responses to the problems posed by typical retrieval tools. User-appropriate chunking of the collection, user control over depth of penetration, and user-determined vocabulary are some of the elements that make reference and browsing powerful tools. The absence of these elements in typical retrieval systems is, in large part, the reason for their failure.

Is there any value, then, to having document representation systems? The answer, of course, is yes. Indeed, there are several parts to an affirmative response. These include:

- Even older systems work for those who know them (e.g., librarians)

- Many searchers have questions that easily fit system constraints

- Digital environments provide for very sophisticated formal systems

- Collection size and time still constrain browsing and reference

Before we explore means for involving the searcher in the representation of questions and documents, we must elaborate upon a distinction and consider some caveats. We must make a distinction between representation that takes place before the searcher comes to the document collection and representation that takes place, at least in part, after the searcher has engaged the collection. Descriptive terms for these two sorts of representation have been developed in the realm of indexing. We can broaden the usage to include both the pointing and the summarizing functions—indexing and abstracting.

Pre-coordinate representation rests upon the indexer/abstractor constructing precise descriptions of document concepts. All the burden for description is at this point. This means that there is no burden on the searcher other than identifying the sanctioned description that suits the request. If the representation of documents is in close accord with user requirements and conventions, then rapid access to appropriate documents is possible. Library of Congress Subject Headings are one well-known pre-coordinate system.

Post-coordinate representation is accomplished, in part, by the user. Elements that are generally simpler in construction than those in pre-coordinate systems are refined and combined by the searcher. The user need not guess a precise string of words. Simple extraction of terms for Boolean combinations, such as one finds in DIALOG searching, is a well-known post-coordinate system. Other post-coordinate systems engage the user by enabling weighting of request elements.

Comparison of Requests

Suppose I wanted to find some works on the "disputes and the ideas for cooperative resource management" for rivers in the West, particularly the Missouri River. Perhaps I could restate my interests in terms such as: "western water law and management" or "law and politics of interstate water allocation." What might a request to the retrieval system look like in Library of Congress Subject Heading terms, in Boolean terms, and in a weighted request system?

Remember that in a pre-coordinate system, I must come up with a word or string of words just like that constructed by the indexer. I might try terms constructed from the primary words in my self-description of my need. Terms such as "cooperative resource management" and "interstate water allocation" would seem natural. However, they would not retrieve a test document on this topic: *River of Promise, River of Peril: The Politics of Managing the Missouri River* by John F. Thorson (Lawrence: University Press of Kansas, 1994).

If I were to think in terms of the Missouri River, I would be successful. The river's name, with a qualifier describing my area of interest, is one of the headings applied to this book in the Library of Congress Cataloging-in-Publication data (found on the copyright page in many books). It is also possible that if I had generalized my search to "water" and had skimmed through all the entries, I would have come across a heading on "water supply" that would have been satisfactory. The three Library of Congress Subject Headings applied to this work are:

1.   Water-supply—Political aspects—Missouri River Watershed

2.   Missouri River Watershed—water rights

3.   Federal-state controversies—United States

The searcher with adequate time and the knowledge that the system operates with very specific descriptors might try variations on original word combinations or might try generalizing (e.g., from "interstate water allocation" to "water"). However, several pieces of research over the past few decades indicate that most searchers will not go to significant lengths to change a query once it has been composed.[1] Of course, it is now common to make use of a computer to search for titles with a specific word or set of words and to avoid the subject heading search as an initial motive. Yet, this assumes that a title will actually contain the word the searcher assumes would be in a title.

In a Boolean post-coordinate system I would be able to say to the system "find all the works in the collection that have been described by all of the following terms." The system would then seek each and every work with each of the terms and then determine the overlap, as in figure 7.1. Again, the terms are likely to be simpler. I might say, "Find works described by 'water' AND 'law' AND 'management'"—these terms could be presented in any order. I might wish to try "river" in place of "water"; or I might say, "I would like anything you have that would be described by either 'river' or 'water,' so long as it is also described by my other terms also." This would yield a query: water OR river AND law AND management. It might also be desirable to limit the search, saying "only show me things printed more recently than five years ago"; or "in the United States, but NOT in the East."

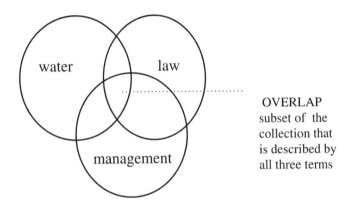

Fig. 7.1. Overlap of collection subsets in a Boolean search.

We must still remember that such a system relies on the documents having previously been described. However, the simple terminology enables the use of computers, thus enabling rapid description by numerous terms. In most weighted descriptor systems, I would be presented with the option to list the terms I thought would be applicable to my search, then to say to what degree each of them was important. For example, I might say that I am very interested in rivers, so I would give it a weight (on a scale of 1 to 10) of 9 or 10. It is also very important to me that politics and management issues be included, so I would weight these with 8 or 9. If the rivers are located in the West, that would be good, but I will look at almost anything, so I might weight "west" with a 6. I might also be able to say that inclusion of photographs is helpful but not particularly important, so perhaps a weight of 4 would be appropriate.

Before I came to the collection, an indexing system weighted all the terms that apply to every document in the collection. Most of the documents may well have absolutely nothing to do with rivers or the West or the law. They will have weights of 0 for these terms. Other works may be travelogues and speak of beautiful rivers in New Hampshire or resource management in national forests. These will have some small overlap with my request. So too will works on politics and ecology, but many of these will be too broad and talk about resources globally or the history of congressional action on national parks.

Then there will be a group of works that has to do with rivers and resource management and law. Some of these will be directly on my topic and others will have considerable overlap but also a broader scope or a narrower scope. The weighting of terms should accomplish two important goals:

- Locate all the works described in much the same way as my request

- Generate a ranking of how close each of the works in the collection is to my query

The ranking will essentially tell me the likelihood that I will be satisfied by each and every one of the documents in the collection. I would probably want to check any documents of 90 percent or greater likelihood first, but I would be free to continue down the ranking if the "best" works were not available or proved too narrow. Weighted systems eliminate the binary retrieval problem. There is no longer a need for a perfect match between a request and a document description. The system does not say: "There was no perfect match to your query, so there are no works to put into your hands. Try a different approach."

Although it is not necessary that post-coordinate systems be built within digital environments (indeed, they were invented in the paper environment), they are certainly enhanced in computer-based systems. A wide variety of approaches to computer-assisted description and retrieval are in various stages of research and implementation. Hybrid combinations of systems are becoming common, sometimes just by ad hoc usage. Many search engines for the Internet present weighted lists of retrieved documents.

As searchers moved away from subject searches as their initial approach, in favor of keyword searches, they discovered that it can be very useful to go back to the subject search with the heading from a work discovered by keyword and say to the system: "Find me more like this one." The system can then look for the subject heading and retrieve documents that do not have the keyword in the title but are, nonetheless, on the topic.

Machine-Augmented Representation

Machine representation of documents provides an opportunity to examine in detail the theory and mechanics of rule-based indexing and abstracting. The manner in which humans represent documents is less subject to careful scrutiny because of the individual and interior nature of the processes involved. Also, humans are often under system constraints that do not allow for consistent application of a set of rules. Still, a close examination of a simple example of computer generation of a representation provides a touchstone for consideration of the conceptual mechanics of representation.

Use of Discontinuities

When we read a book or an article, we are constantly making distinctions between the background and the squiggles of ink. We are also grouping squiggles into letters, distinguishing one letter from the next, and distinguishing one word from the next. All of these activities may be described as observing discontinuities in the data stream.

Bateson suggests that information is a "difference that makes a difference."[2] First, we have to detect a discontinuity—the difference between the medium of the message and the squiggles, then between each of the squiggles, then between clusters of squiggles. Then we must make some determination of how much of a difference is significant. Figure 7.2 models the general concept of detecting points of difference in the data that are input to the patron.

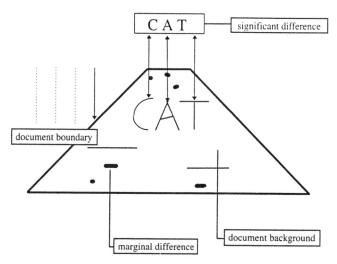

Fig. 7.2. Seeking differences that make a difference. The terms *marginal* and *significant* are used here for the ordinary case. These evaluative terms could be changed in some instances.

If we encounter the cluster of squiggles "the," we know that this is an individual cluster, generally because there is a blank space on either side of it. The cluster "the" is handy as a little pointer, but has little meaningful content on its own. That item to which "the" points is generally the meaningful term, so, once it is encountered, "the" is put aside. It is a difference that makes little, if any, difference.

Suppose that the cluster following "the" is "buffalo." This cluster does not appear as frequently in most texts as "the," and therefore it is a candidate for making a difference. Once we decode the cluster, the actual determination of difference takes place. If the cluster "buffalo" appears fairly frequently in a text, it will probably represent a meaningful concept. If it is seen too frequently, it may actually lose some of its difference-making ability. One could imagine a book of uses of buffalo on the Great Plains, which listed buffalo bones, buffalo blood, buffalo tail, buffalo horns, buffalo heart, buffalo hide, buffalo hair, and so on. Once the book had been found, "buffalo" would be too broad a term to distinguish aspects of use of the animal.

Clearly, different circumstances will determine just how much difference is made by any set of squiggles. Just as clearly, the squiggles remain fixed—they are the major diachronic attributes. We can assume that a person indexing or abstracting a document is presented with the same stream of data from the page (or the analog in other media) as any other reader. The person making an index or abstract must determine some level of difference that will be significant. Then, when differences at or above that level are detected, the indexer/abstracter must decode them and give them a conceptual tag—the index term or abstract.

The problems of indeterminacy—times when the system's representation of a document is not appropriate for a patron who would have been pleased with the document—are founded largely in the detecting and tagging of differences. If so much depends on detecting discontinuities in the data stream, perhaps we should simply:

- Detect the points of difference

- Say how big they are

- Say where they are

- Let the patron determine the significance

In fact, this is the basis for machine indexing and abstracting. Most work in machine representation of documents has been conducted on word-based documents, though the burgeoning interest in multimedia documents has begun to yield models for machine-based representation of image and sound documents.

Computers store text files by having a string of 1s and 0s stand for each letter and each punctuation mark in the text. Each 1 or 0 represents an electrical state of on or off and is termed a *bit*. The ASCII (American Standard Code for Information Interchange) seven-bit code, a standard representation for letters, uses a seven-place string for each letter. A computer program can use this code to examine each and every character in a text. By looking for the code that represents the blank space, the program can cluster letters into words. By counting how frequently the words appear in the text, the program can produce a measure of the size of the difference that cluster has compared to the text as a whole.

In practice, we know from studies of frequencies of word occurrences that many words are unlikely to be meaningful to most system users. Such words are often included in the program so that when the computer detects them, they are simply left out of consideration. *Stop list* (sometimes termed a *kill list*) is the general term for this part of a program. Table 7.1 lists the terms in a typical stop list, which are likely to be of little utility to most users of the program. Notice that the major portion comprises pronouns, articles, prepositions, forms of the verb "to be," and adjectives. In many instances, though certainly not all, these words do little to represent topics.

Extraction is the most common form of machine representation of documents. The representation highlighting rule is simply "present all words that are not on the stop list." It is common to make additions, such as:

- Alphabetize the words

- Tell how many times each word appears

- Arrange the words by frequency

- Give the address of each word

- Show the words on either side of the selected word

It is also possible to extract words not by frequency, but by:

- Where they appear in the document (title, opening or closing sentence, etc.)

- Type of word (noun, verb, adjective)

- Emphasis by bolding or italics

Table 7.1
Sample Stop List

```
DATA the,a,can,may,of,in,with,and,without,get,is,are
DATA The,May,A, Is, Are, Were, Because,Will,If,Let, For, Most
DATA Be, While, An, Between,Had, How, It, Also,On,One, Some
DATA There, This, Typically, Usually, What, Which, All, Our, Not
DATA be, were, because, will, if, let, or, for, I, most, out, until
DATA Within, Up, Would, These, But,Routinely, Often, Another
DATA Now, Their, We, When, After, Always, He
DATA while, an, any, been, between, by, cannot, do, etc, far,faster
DATA from, given, had, has, have, how, it, also, might, more, much
DATA no, on, one, other, same, some, than, that, them, there, this
DATA to, too, two, typically, usually, what, which, all, our, as, per
DATA well, so, at, again, merely, use,recently,over
DATA even, whether, however, along, upon, particular, therefore, unless
DATA they, ought,not,within,up,whole,would, these,but, its, each
DATA require, could,yet, routinely,often, very,large, numerous,recent
DATA another, little, almost, thus,among, currently, indeed, many, now
DATA we,when, about,after,always,easily,generally,good, greatly
DATA he, hence,highly,his,her,into,just,latest,likely
DATA must,ones,only,put,says, should,something,their,then,thing,those
DATA three,totally,where,whereas,you,your,youre, able,wholly,whose
DATA Rd, OF, ON, OR,Needless, No,My,Mr,Mrs, MY,IN,His,Her, Ave
DATA am,became,being,did,him,me,my,she,us,who, whither,Upon,under
DATA,Each,both,first,make,through, Do,doing,Yet,yet,Why,So,so,Such
DATA Dr,was,shall,depends,mere,affords,thee, yield,especially,seeks,confer
DATA rather,resulted,suggested,commenced,partly,Other,proceeded,exist
DATA contains, affect,chief,means,existing,nor,following,whatever,addition
DATA begun,principally,laid,passed,around,occasionally,ourselves,happen
DATA To,arrived,here,already,towards,gives,become,try,preceding
DATA every,hitherto,Its,seeming,never,before,You,made,early,fix,began
DATA supposing,commence,induce,consistent,forever,itself ,various,And
DATA want,Wherefore,undoubtedly,watching,went,Your,yours,whenever
DATA theirs,turned,trifling,taken,themselves,Those,sufficiently,suddenly,
DATA see,said,seen,say,steady,supposed,saw,still,several,soon,since,some
DATA someone,still,shall,slowly,suppose,scarcely,returned,replied,proceed
DATA preferred, perhaps,practically,probable,picked,preceeded,meet,near
DATA others,owes,open,once,otherwise,off,Only,Once,latter,like,keeping
DATA instantly,In,having,herself,Here,himself,greater,going,greatest,give
```

Extraction can be augmented by using a thesaurus to bring words for the same concept together and including them all in the frequency count. It is also possible to use a thesaurus to translate terms to a sanctioned list of terms. Such approaches require careful consideration of the patrons, because these approaches reintroduce the issues of conceptual tagging and translation.

Abstracts can be produced with an extension of the extraction method of representation: Simply extract whole sentences by finding punctuation marks. The rule for finding those sentences could be either "select sentences by where they appear" or "select sentences that contain the most frequently appearing words on the list of extracted terms." Especially in technical literature, where editorial policies tend to enforce format, extraction by location is not as haphazard as it might seem initially. If, for example, the first paragraph must contain the hypothesis of the research and the next-to-the-last paragraph must contain summary results, then location is not difficult.

Systems based on extraction remove the barrier of an intermediary constructing concepts and their tags from the document data stream. They filter out the elements least likely to be of significance and allow the patron to determine depth of penetration. However, they do not directly include the patron's information requirement in the making of the rule for highlighting. Such systems also cannot account for synchronic changes. Future searchers might not understand the terminology or references of the author.

Sophisticated versions of machine representation are constantly being developed and tested. It is beyond the scope of this chapter to consider these, but we will return to additional methods for word (text) documents and for multimedia documents as we consider more sophisticated representation rules.

An Elementary Word-Extraction Program

Examining an elementary extraction program will enhance understanding of both the binary representation of words and the application of rule-based representation to word-based texts. Our sample text is displayed in figure 7.3. We will follow the steps of a program designed to:

- Extract from the document any words not on our stop list

- Alphabetize the words on the list of extracted terms

- Calculate the frequency with which the terms appear

- Provide an address within the test for each word

Figure 7.4 on page 102 presents the general flow of the extraction portion of the program. It presents segments of the ASCII seven-bit binary code, with the numbers translated into decimal form for ease of reading. Extraction depends on comparison of each character to the ASCII code to determine if it is a letter—a significant difference for our purposes. When this first level of difference determination is accomplished, letter clusters (words) are then compared to the stop list to ensure that we extract only clusters of sufficiently significant difference. In outline form the flow is:

- Open the text file

- Do everything below as long as there are characters in the text file

- Input one character

- Check to see if that character is a blank or a letter

- If it is a letter, add it to the string that will become a word

- If it is a blank space, pick up the word string

- Compare the word string with each word in the stop list

- If there is a match, empty the word string and return to input

- If there is not a match, store the word for later use

- Empty the word string and return to input

PhD in Library and Information Management

theory core

Information Engineering
Informational Psychology
Sociology of Information
Information Organization Management

Each doctoral student will construct a program of advanced coursework and substantial research on a foundation of theory drawn from these fields. A faculty dedicated to both research and instruction, a curriculum both rigorous and congenial, and a nurturing academic community will foster student abilities to contribute to society's understanding of the creation, diffusion, and utilization of information.

Each student will first acquire the theoretical concepts and research abilities associated with a master's degree program.

In close consultation with appropriate faculty members, each student will be challenged to investigate and develop theory within these aspects of the Library and Information Management discipline:

Aesthetics; Contexts of Use; Dynamics of Human Systems; Culture; Engineering; Management; Policy; Visualization; Organizational Design; Economics; Values and Ethics

Substantial course and laboratory work will be devoted to developing expertise in the selection of research topics, methodologies, implementation, data analysis, and reporting.

Cognate coursework in related fields will strengthen the theory base and research capabilities of each doctoral student.

An advanced seminar in graduate-level teaching or in managerial issues will enhance each graduate's ability to make a substantial contribution to the discipline and to society.

Each doctoral candidate will contribute new knowledge to the field through the writing and public defense of a dissertation.

Fig. 7.3. Sample document for computerized extraction example.

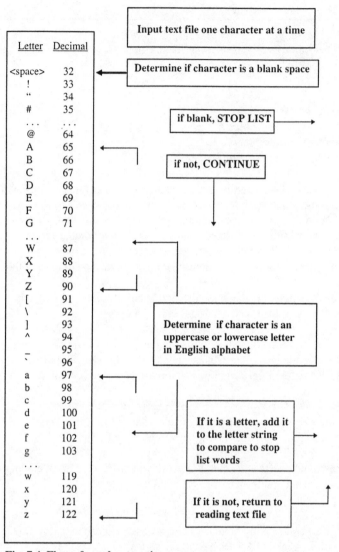

Fig. 7.4. Flow of word-extraction program.

For those interested in pursuing the program further, the appendix lists the primary pieces of code for the program in QBASIC. These simple pieces of code should offer a basis for exploring word extraction for beginning programmers.

All these steps combine to yield a list of terms that do not appear on the stop list. A similar set of steps alphabetizes the words and counts how many times each one is found in the text. The sort routine could also be set to order terms by frequency of occurrence, though that has not been done for this example. The alphabetic sorting of our sample text is presented in table 7.2. The frequency of each word is given in parentheses following the word. Note that this sort uses ASCII order, so that all words beginning with uppercase letters are alphabetized first.

Table 7.2.
Keywords from Figure 7.3 Alphabetized with Frequency
of Occurrence.

Contexts(1)	Culture(1)	Design(1)	Dynamics(1)
Economics(1)	Engineering(2)	Ethics(1)	Human(1)
Information(5)	Informational(1)	Library(2)	Management(4)
Organization(1)	Organizational(1)	PhD(1)	Policy(1)
Psychology(1)	Sociology(1)	Substantial(1)	Systems(1)
Use(1)	Values(1)	Visualization(1)	abilities(2)
ability(1)	academic(1)	acquire(1)	advanced(2)
analysis(1)	appropriate(1)	aspects(1)	associated(1)
base(1)	candidate(1)	capabilities(1)	challenged(1)
close(1)	community(1)	concepts(1)	congenial(1)
construct(1)	consultation(1)	contribute(2)	contribution(1)
core(1)	course(1)	coursework(2)	creation(1)
curriculum(1)	data(1)	dedicated(1)	defense(1)
degree(1)	develop(1)	developing(1)	devoted(1)
diffusion(1)	discipline(2)	dissertation(1)	doctoral(3)
drawn(1)	enhance(1)	expertise(1)	faculty(2)
field(1)	fields(2)	foster(1)	foundation(1)
graduate(1)	graduates(1)	implementation(1)	information(1)
instruction(1)	investigate(1)	issues(1)	knowledge(1)
laboratory(1)	level(1)	managerial(1)	masters(1)
members(1)	methodology(1)	new(1)	nurturing(1)
program(2)	public(1)	related(1)	reporting(1)
research(5)	rigorous(1)	selection(1)	seminar(1)
society(1)	society[']s(1)	strengthen(1)	student(5)
substantial(2)	teaching(1)	theoretical(1)	theory(4)
topics(1)	understand(1)	utilization(1)	work(1)
writing(1)			

One striking attribute of this list is its size (105 words), even with a stop list of more than 500 terms and a one-page document as the text. Even with the removal of prepositions, many adjectives, and many verb forms, there is a substantial set of significantly different clusters of squiggles. Upon examination of the words extracted by this first pass, we may want to add some of them to the stop list. Some of the words on the list will be of limited utility that we just had not thought of ahead of time.

More vexing is the separation of terms that would normally be more meaningful if taken together, such as: "Information" + "Management"; "Information" + "Engineering"; "academic" + "community"; and "faculty" + "member." It would be possible to write subroutines to take care of some of these problem cases. It is also quite realistic to think of the computer serving as the tool to make the first pass, enabling the information professional to make adjustments and enhancements based on a working knowledge of the clientele.

There is also the issue of gathering together terms that appear in both the upper- and lowercase lists, such as "Information" and "information," as well as the different forms of a word, such as "Organization" and "Organizational." Such issues point up the fact that even a machine environment does not make problems disappear. However, it does make certain problems evident and offer possible solutions.

Table 7.3 presents only the terms that appear two or more times. In addition to the frequency of appearance, the table lists the address of the words. Clearly, this is a much shorter list (17 words, or about 16 percent of the complete list) and the terms are what one would expect in a document about a new doctoral program in "information" "management" with a "substantial" focus on "students" and their acquisition of a rigorous grounding in "theory" and "research." Filtering out the terms appearing more than two times yields a list that could be a standard set of descriptive terms.

- Information(5)
- Management(4)
- doctoral(3)
- research(5)
- student(5)
- theory(4)

Making the other terms available to those with further interest enables deeper levels of representation of the details of the document.

Table 7.3.
Extracted Words from Figure 7.3 with Frequencies of at Least Two

Engineering(2)	76, 1014
Library(2)	9, 892
Management(4)	33, 173, 916, 1028
Information(5)	21, 64, 130, 144, 904
abilities(2)	494, 682
advanced(2)	238, 1442
contribute(2)	507, 1652
coursework(2)	247, 1321
discipline(2)	928, 1593
faculty(2)	341, 777
fields(2)	330, 1343
program(2)	227, 726
substantial(2)	264, 1559
doctoral(3)	193, 1418, 1628
theory(4)	48, 304, 855, 1370
research(5)	276, 367, 671, 1225, 1388
student(5)	202, 486, 615, 799, 1427

A one-page document is not a realistic test of a system; however, it does present the potential, as well as some of the challenges, offered by the digital environment.[3] It should be noted that extraction of the terms, even in the modified slow version of the program running on a home computer, requires much less than one minute. Sorting and counting frequencies likewise take only a few seconds.

The reason for attending to this exercise in machine representation is not simply to compare human and machine indexing. Rather, it is to demonstrate the potential utility of representing the structural attributes of the physically present text, that is, the discontinuities in the data stream. The machine environment enables precise attention to detail and the rapid multiple application of simple rules. This yields an ability to present complex constructs.

Precise measurement and manipulation allow the computer to provide contour maps of documents. The rules of representation can be specified and made known, just as are the rules for geographical contour maps. Different users can make different uses of different levels of detail in the maps. The rules can even be modified according to patron needs.

Most importantly, the making of conceptual tags is eliminated or significantly reduced. This results in removing the responsibility of constructing a conceptual tag from the indexer or abstracter and barriers from the patron.

Notes

1.   See the discussion of "anchoring" in Blair, particularly pages 14 to 19 and 40 to 41. David C. Blair, *Language and Representation in Information Retrieval* (New York: Elsevier, 1990).

2.   Gregory Bateson, *Mind and Nature: A Necessary Unity* (New York: E. P. Dutton, 1979).

3.   There are, of course, cautions to be heeded in automation. Stoll raises provocative issues in his *Silicon Snake Oil* that require serious consideration, lest the digital environment become an arcane and sterile environment. See Cliff Stoll, *Silicon Snake Oil: Second Thoughts on the Information Highway* (New York: Doubleday, 1995).

Chapter 8
Depth of Representation

The level of specificity at which documents are represented largely determines the patron's depth of penetration into the document collection, as well as the individual documents. Unless the patron actually obtains each document and determines depth of penetration, the system's representation is the only window available. We have made the case, through exercises and models, that representing at the level of the document may well keep a wealth of material hidden from users. We have also examined a very simple model of computer representation of a tiny document as a possible approach to returning some control over depth of representation to the patron.

Browsing has been posited as a response to some of the difficulties posed by having an external agency set a single level of specificity, among other things. Machine-assisted representation is one approach to imbuing a system's representation of documents with some of the dynamic rules for highlighting found in browsing. The possibilities and problems of machine representation bear further consideration. Issues of scale are particularly important. What happens when we use our simple word-extraction program on a text of more typical size?

We need a framework for elaborating our considerations of machine-augmented representation. Before reading further in this book, return to chapter 6, "Responses to Subject Indeterminacy." Read through the chapter and construct a set of descriptors for it. Here we will consider several sets of representations of that chapter, with special emphasis on the performance of the computer program used in chapter 7. The machine's performance will be evaluated within the context of breadth and depth.

A touchstone for our considerations of machine indexing was established by an indexer working with the prepublication manuscript of the article on which chapter 6 is based.[1] The letter in figure 8.1 highlights that operation. The indexer timed a single, close reading for comparison with the time it would require the machine to read through the text and extract terms. In round figures, that comparison is just over three minutes for the computer and a little over an hour for the indexer.

At the end of the computer's run, all the words not on the stop list had been extracted. At the end of the indexer's reading, the final decisions of what to highlight had yet to be made. It did take the computer another half-minute to sort all the extracted terms into alphabetical order and tabulate frequencies of occurrence for each term.

It is critical to note the phrase "I finally decided upon." The rules for extraction generally are not explicit in the process of most human indexing. There is, in saying this, no value judgment of the quality of the representation made by the indexer. It is simply important to note that it may be difficult or impossible for a human indexer to specify the exact mechanism he or she used for highlighting. It may well be that personal knowledge of the types of users of the system will enable very good representations. However, we are left without any method of addressing issues of consistency across time and across settings.

We must remember that inter-indexer consistency is not necessarily a desirable system characteristic. Indexing that is consistent but not useful to patrons does not constitute a good representation system. Also, it is possible to imagine a situation in which one of several indexers is consistently different from all the others, but in so being, is consistently representing documents in a manner hospitable to a particular type of user.

When we speak here of consistency, as offered by a computer environment, we are speaking of a system for which the rules of extraction are known (or can be made known) to the patron and in which the approach to extraction is consistent. The approach to extraction may well be (ought to be) tunable to each use. A representation of a document ought to be based on the information needs and the decoding abilities of the patron, as we have suggested. This likely means that there will be significant inconsistency in the system across uses by different patrons or even the same patron at different times. However, there would be consistency in presenting to each patron the palette of attributes most appropriate to that patron.

A good reference librarian or on-line search intermediary often takes the time to elicit the bounds of the question state and the decoding capabilities of the patron. A selection of potentially useful works will probably be presented to the patron for evaluation. This form of representation of documents approaches the customized constructions implied by the definitions of representation that we have used.

Two difficulties arise, however. There is the possibility that external constraints will impose a different level of service for different patrons. Different reference librarians or searchers may have more or less skill in eliciting representation requirements and in translating those into effective searches. Even the same intermediary at different times may well perform differently.[2] Also, so long as representation tools are constructed before they are used, the human librarian or search intermediary is constrained to use those a priori representations or to operate on personal knowledge of documents. Although they may have a better working knowledge of the subtleties of representation practices than a patron, they are still operating at whatever level of penetration and with whatever tagging of concepts have been provided by somebody else.

I have read the article only once, although I am familiar
with some of the related readings you cited. I did not use
any particular thesaurus of terms [for this stage]. . . . It took
me a little more than one hour to read the article, but I was
reading closely, rather than skimming. . . .

Here are the terms I finally decided on. (Note—these are
in no particular order. . . . I could weight them if you think
that would be helpful. Those which I consider to be most
important are asterisked.)

- * Browsing
- Topical description
- * Document representation
- * Document retrieval
- Indexing
- * Search process
- Access methods
- Computer-assisted searching
- Anomalous state of knowledge

One topic [for which] I couldn't come up with an
appropriate term . . . is:
> "incongruence between searcher's terms and
> document representations in the bibliographical
> system."

I also debated . . . whether the types and stages of browsing
should be included (expansion, vague awareness,
monitoring, knowledge creation; make glimpses, connect
attributes, evaluate connections, evaluate search). . . . It
seems that these headings and stages could also be
transmuted into index terms which may be useful to
someone. However, the terms by themselves are so
ambiguous that I wonder whether they would only
contribute to false hits rather than add anything meaningful
to the document representation.

Fig. 8.1. Part of letter from indexer about article on which chapter 6 was based.

Of course, talented humans will be capable of making rich and subtle representations tailored to individuals. However, much of that effort might be accomplished with greater facility by incorporation of machine augmentation of the extracting and sorting processes. Rapid accomplishment of almost unimaginably large numbers of small steps is the forte of the machine system. Humans involved in representation are likely to be constrained by time. Thus, general-level representation often results not from a lack of ability, nor because of theoretical necessity, but from too little time to carry out the number of iterations of steps necessary for greater depth.

The list of terms provided by the indexer of the browsing article (see again figure 8.1) is nine items long. No suggestions were made to the indexer about depth or breadth. On the list provided, we note that the items marked with asterisks are full document descriptors. Those not so marked are at levels of generality above and below that of the whole document. The terms "indexing" and "access methods" include much more than is covered in chapter 6. Belkin's term "anomalous state of knowledge" is important, but it is, clearly, only one way of describing the psychological state that might stimulate browsing activity. The other two terms, "topical description" and "computer-assisted searching," are similarly specific.

The concept of "incongruence between a searcher's terms and document representations in the bibliographic system" is central to the article/chapter that was indexed. This is the primary reason for browsing, and it is the framework for constructing alternative models of the search process. The difficulty expressed in the indexer's note reflects the difficulty in tagging concepts. The concept has been identified, but coding it in a manner that is both expressive and manipulable proved to be difficult. Using "incongruity" by itself leaves open the possibility of many "false drops"—users coming to the document on the promise of the representation, only to be disappointed that the concept is not used in an expected or useful manner. Making evident the relationship between the user and the bibliographic system brings one back to the long expression. The indexer insightfully notes that the same situation holds for the terms describing types and stages of browsing activity.

Again, we must point out that this is good indexing in the traditional sense. These representations are sufficient to many uses. The indexer did not attempt to do a mediocre representation, nor should we find any fault with the effort. Yet the indexer's own insights and frustrations with system inadequacies are evident in the notes accompanying the list of terms. This frustration reflects the lack of subtlety available to indexers in the attempt to provide powerful tools to patrons.

Machine Representation Results

The extraction and sorting program used in this chapter is based on the program fragments presented earlier in chapter 7 and also used in the appendix. It is a very simple program and does not incorporate many of the sophisticated methods of textual analysis that have been developed over the last several years. It is, however, instructive in both its speed of operation and the results it produces.

These results point to the promise of machine augmentation of representation, while also pointing to some of the problems that have had to be resolved in order for computers to construct useful tools. Table 8.1 (on page 117) is a printout of the extracted terms in the order of their extraction. Table 8.2 (on page 136) is a listing of the words after they were alphabetized and counted. Note that table 8.2 contains words that are truncated for memory management purposes. Both tables contain some typographic errors from the original text, such as "bserved" instead of "observed."

The most immediately obvious difference between the indexer's list of terms and the computer's list of terms is sheer size. If we count only the terms on the indexer's primary list, there are 9; on the computer's list, 2,657. The indexer's list is less than 3 percent of the size of the machine's list, even though there is a stop list of more than 500 words that are excluded from consideration.

In and of itself, this difference in size does not necessarily mean that the computer-generated list is better. In fact, the indexer's comment about "false hits" and manageability are severely magnified. The first step we want to take in considering the machine results is to examine the entries closely. The first pass of the text through the program made use of the existing stop list. Yet, there is nothing magical about that stop list. It was developed from looking at words commonly found in stop lists and adding others as various texts were run through it. The current text is likely to point out necessary additions.

A close look at this first pass is instructive. As we noted in the earlier chapter, words beginning with uppercase letters are alphabetized as a group, followed by all words beginning with lowercase letters. This has two immediate effects. Any words that occur in both the upper- and lowercase groups are not grouped together here. If this were deemed important (and it likely would be in most systems), we would want to remove case sensitivity from the counting routine. Also, any words that are on the stop list in lowercase form will not prevent an uppercase form of that word from showing up on the extraction list. Thus, "for" might be on the stop list, but "For" would be extracted because the ASCII numeric representation of "F" (70) is different from that of "f" (102).

Having said these things about the list of extracted and sorted words, let us go through the list to find words that should be put onto the stop list because they are of little value to our current text, and likely to other texts. The stop list is available for examination by users, so any word on the list can be removed for particular searches. Candidate terms for inclusion on the stop list are:

- Nouns and adjectival or noun forms of verbs that are too general to offer discrimination capabilities to a patron include: Achieving, Activity, Adding, Figure, Using, act, affiliation, containing, getting, giving, holding, implying, importance, initiating, intent, leading, leanings, license, looking, making, nothing, parts, possibility, proposition, putting, ranging, removing, requirement, standing, start, starting, stepping, striking, taking, task, tending, throwing, troubling, varying, way, ways.

- Proper names offer an interesting challenge. For many patrons, they simply add to the clutter; for others, the presence of a familiar name can be an important clue to the contents and, perhaps, the line of thinking behind the contents. Because the names on our list appear only infrequently, we might want to leave them in and consider means to make them evident when necessary.

- More than 60 articles, particles, prepositions (except "of"[3]), adverbs, and general adjectives were, for some reason, not on the original stop list: Any, Clearly, Different, Earlier, First, Fine, Herein, However, Just, NOT ("Not" and "not" are on the stop list, but this emphatic spelling had not been anticipated), Short, Similarly, Single, Subsequent, Therefore, Three, above, active, adequate, aside, available, awry, best, beyond, chosen, clearly, closely, common, concisely, considerable, countless, current, either, entire, entirely, equally, exactly, extremely, fairly, fill, four, frequent, fruitful, full, fully, further, general, half, hard, high, immediately, important, incidentally, individual, indiviual (typographic errors are just character strings to the machine), interesting, less, likewise, long, maybe, mostly, nearby, normally, precisely, properly, subsequent, tantamount, why.

In general, verbs and adverbs are excluded by the stop list because they are not directly linked to concepts. Some verbs, such as "catalyze," "create," and "describe," which are in fact directly linked to concepts, are left on our main list. In addition to the general classes of terms previously listed, which could be included on the stop list for the next run through the program, there are some interesting special cases:

- "Catalyzing" appears only once, but is tied to an important concept.

- "Congress" is actually a part of the phrase "Library of Congress." Thus, we would want to build a subroutine to keep the elements of proper names together.

- "Idols" is part of a title, *Idols of Perversity*. It too should be kept with its kin.

- "Serendipity" appears only once, but is often used as a synonym for *browsing*. Thus, we would want to make it evident, despite its low frequency. Also, we might want to consider whether it should be counted together with "browsing" when determining frequencies.

- "abilities" and "ability" comprise the first of several clusters in our list that are made up of words with the same stem. We would want to consider merging these terms.

- "century" presents the same sort of problem as the compound proper names and titles mentioned earlier, yet with an added difficulty. There are no clues, such as "several words each beginning with uppercase letters" or "uppercase letters not at the beginning of a sentence." With "century," we would have to know beforehand that it sometimes occurs together with a number to denote a particular century, in this case the "nineteenth" (a term that appears later in the list).

- "dumb" (from the phrase "dumb luck") is similar to "century," except that there is the rule "because an adjective is generally connected to a noun, scan for a nearby noun."

- "everything" presents the possibility of a very interesting index entry. This would be a term at a very high level of generality!

- "gullibility" is another word standing for a concept fundamental to browsing, yet because it appears only once in the list, it runs the risk of being excluded from searches by all but the most motivated of patrons.

- "library" and "librarian" appear fewer times than might be expected in an article on browsing. This is because the setting for browsing is generalized to any collection of documents and the subsequent use of more general terms, such as "bibliographic agency."

- "queries" and "questions" happen to fall together within this list, so they can be seen as synonyms and counted together. What, then, are we to do about synonymous words that are in the list, but are not immediately self-evident? Should there be a thesaurus to link the terms? Should the linked terms appear together or have "see also" notes? What if one term is really a subset of another, rather than a synonym at the same level of specificity?

- "stream" appears five times, a relatively high frequency. Yet it is used only metaphorically for a three-dimensional and time-varying model in the source document. Would a patron looking for material on bodies of water be happy to find this document?

Having discussed the list and the shortcomings that we might want to address, we should now look at the possibilities presented by the frequency counts, which the program tabulated during the sorting routine. The frequencies give us a means of setting the depth of penetration into the collection. If we wished, we could say that only terms appearing with a particular frequency or greater will be used as descriptors. However, we saw earlier, in our discussion of optimal depth, that there is no way for a system to set a depth that will be satisfactory to all users. Instead, we can make available all of the extracted terms, with the frequencies used as a depth gauge, as in figure 8.2.

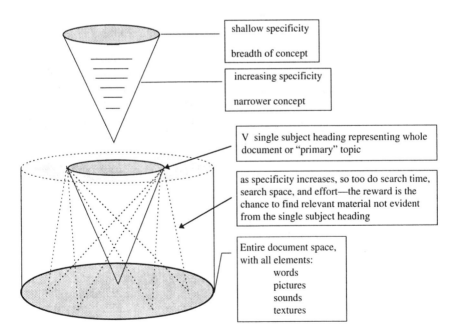

shallow specificity

breadth of concept

increasing specificity

narrower concept

V single subject heading representing whole document or "primary" topic

as specificity increases, so too do search time, search space, and effort—the reward is the chance to find relevant material not evident from the single subject heading

Entire document space, with all elements:
    words
    pictures
    sounds
    textures

Fig. 8.2. User control of depth of penetration enables searching beyond the primary subject heading without resorting to mere random search.

Setting the depth gauge at different levels yields compelling results. We see, at the highest level of generality, a set of terms very much like what we would expect of a human indexer with a system constraint to apply a handful of terms at the level of the document. As we set the depth gauge at lower thresholds, we see elements from deeper within the document begin to appear.

In our list of terms extracted from the source document, the most frequent terms occur 43, 47, and 49 times. If we were to cluster terms beginning with both upper- and lowercase versions of the same letter, or if we were to cluster "search" and "searcher," we would get somewhat higher figures. If we take 40 as our first depth reading, we are saying "show only the terms that appeared very frequently, and therefore ought to be associated in some strong way with the major concepts of the document." High frequency is indicative of broad concepts rather than details. The output presented in figure 8.3 is the subset of terms derived by setting the depth at its shallowest level of penetration.

```
begin sort of 2657 terms at: 01:22:13
end sort of 2657 terms at:   01:22:39

alpha sort of file "brzchp" showing words appearing > 40


                    attributes    ( 49 )
                    document      ( 47 )
                    search        ( 43 )


          total terms in list      3
```

Fig. 8.3. Output of sort-and-tabulate routine with depth set at "shallow."

The article and chapter are about browsing as a search method that optimizes connection of user attributes and document attributes, so figure 8.3 presents a fair representation. The only elements conspicuously absent are "browsing" and "user." If we combine the upper- and lowercase forms of "browsing," as in figure 8.4, then the total number of appearances of the word is more than 40 and it would appear on this list. Similarly, if we were to combine the totals for "search" and "searcher" and put both words on the list, we would bring a synonym for "user" into the broad output.

```
begin sort of 2657 terms at: 01:22:13
end sort of 2657 terms at:   01:22:39

alpha sort of file "brzchp" showing words appearing > 40


                    attributes     ( 49 )
                    [B]browsing    ( 42 )
                    document       ( 47 )
                    search         ( 43 )


          total terms in list       4
```

Fig. 8.4. Output as in figure 8.3, but with two forms of "browsing" combined, yielding a total large enough for inclusion at this level.

Alternatively, we could set the depth gauge to its next level and pick up "searcher" (38), as well as "collection" (36) and the plural form "documents" (38). In the shallow range, there are so few terms that we increment the depth (the threshold) in steps of five. In fact, there is no change in list membership when we move from a threshold of 35 to a setting of 30; both lists have the same six terms.

As we move the depth indicator to 25, we pick up the lowercase "browsing." We are still at a relatively shallow depth, so that even without combining forms of the word it will show up as a descriptor in many searches. Moving down to what might be termed the bottom of the shallow zone, we begin to see changes.

By setting the depth at 20, we pick up another four terms: the singular "attribute" (22), "knowledge" (21), "representation" (24), and "scholar" (25). Note that "scholar" appears only on this list rather than the "greater than 25" list because our threshold statement is "any word occurring *more* than the threshold number," which in this case is 20.

Setting the level at 15, as in figure 8.5, brings us to a point where the nature of the list begins to change. The total number of items on the list is now more than four times the size of the first list with its depth of 40. We begin to see more subordinate concepts, such as "connection," "set," "sampling." We also begin to see adjectives, such as "new," and "useful." As these appear with some considerable frequency, a patron might find them useful.

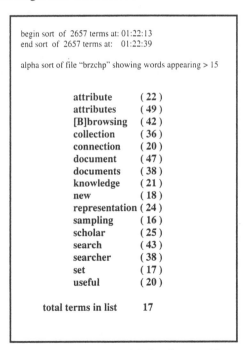

Fig. 8.5. Descriptor list with depth set at 15.

As we increment the depth indicator from level 15 to level 1 in increments of 1, we pick up more and more subordinate concepts and adjectives. The total number of terms on the list increases, of course; slowly at first, but increasing as we approach level 1. At a level of 10, there are 25 terms; at level 7, 46 terms; at level 5,

Such a demonstration suggests that the simple method of counting word frequencies can represent a document in the typical manner of a few terms at the most general level, as well as a manner in which the user can choose the amount of detail (and the consequent amount of effort) that seems appropriate for any particular use. The numbers provide the patron with a contour map of the document terrain; the use and determination of meaning are left to the user.

Frequency figures for each term serve as depth indicators in two ways. If a patron chooses to see all terms extracted from a document, the number of appearances can give an indication of the breadth of the term. If the number is large, the word is used significantly in the document; if it is small, the term probably represents a detail or a subordinate concept. We must point out that the correlation is not always exact. The user and the system must account for:

- Synonyms

- Variant forms of the same word stem

- The possibility of an infrequent word still referring to a significant concept

- Users looking for concepts not necessarily intended by the author

The patron can also determine the level of observation and just examine the descriptor lists at that level. If all works in which a term appears are desired, the threshold will be set very shallow, to cast the broadest net. If works that discuss a concept in some depth are desired, then the threshold can be set with a higher number. This means the term appears frequently and is likely to represent a significant aspect of the text.

Of course, there are systems with much more sophisticated analysis capabilities. It is now possible to take a document that a patron likes, analyze its word frequencies and statistical structure, and then have the computer search all documents in the collection for similar profiles. If the seed document was of use to the patron, then similar documents (presented in a list of ranked degrees of similarity) should also be of use to the patron. Statistical analyses can also lead to concept clusters, rather than just single terms or groups of synonyms. Yet, even the systems with considerably more sophistication than our small example are based on the machine extraction of characters and addresses and frequencies.

Even our small example was able to extract well over 2,000 terms in a matter of minutes; it then sorted the terms and tabulated frequencies in 13 seconds. Even if the system were to be used only by the human indexer, and not directly by the patron, the speed, algorithmic consistency, and possible insights about elements at varying depths make the machine a powerful tool for representation.

Notes

1. Brian O'Connor, "Browsing: A Framework for Seeking Functional Information," *Knowledge: Creativity, Diffusion, Utilization* 15, no. 2 (1993): 211-32.

2. W. S. Cooper, "Is Interindexer Consistency a Deep Hobgoblin?" *American Documentation* 20, no. 3 (July 1969): 100-110.

3. Charles T. Meadow, *Text Information Retrieval Systems* (San Diego, Calif.: Academic Press, 1988). See especially the example and discussion on page 193.

Table 8.1
Extracted Words in Order of Extraction*

Browsing	creative	getting
response	scholarly	shortcomings
subject	work	representation
indeterminacy	requires	external
Earlier	functional	party
explorations	access	leaves
discussed	Farrow	decision
fundamental	OConnor	represented
troubling	unknowabilit	patron
problems	potential	leaves
presented	interactions	depth
patrons	scholars	penetration
articulate	documents	collection
questions	further	indiviual
system	complicates	document
terms	picture	patron
discussed	speaking	tradeoff
Blairs	undiscovered	method
concept	public	requirement
subject	knowledge	patron
indeterminacy	essential	resources
significant	incompleteness	time
likelihood	search	effort
failure	retrieval	Clearly
striking	Swanson	patrons
Subsequent	notes	browsing
discussions	search	option
examined	process	engaged
methods	scientific	creation
enhancing	theory	new
indexing	criticized	knowledge
abstracting	improved	best
moderate	verified	method
likelihood	capable	searching
failure	retrieving	browsing
However	information	form
approaches	relevant	indexing
ability	problem	abstracting
articulate	theory	Representation
small	Browsing	collection
set	set	individual
topics	procedures	documents

* The source used for extraction was the prepublication manuscript of an article later used as the basis of chapter 6: Brian O'Connor, "Browsing: A Framework for Seeking Functional Information," *Knowledge: Creation, Diffusion, Utilization* 15, no. 2 (1993): 211-32. The table shows the contents of the article minus terms from a stop list similar to the list in table 7.1 (page 99).

accomplished
patron
agent
representation
Selection
attributes
takes
place
ad
hoc
priori
patron
control
location
depth
engagement
collection
patron
formulates
rules
highlighting
patron
constructs
coding
system
patron
determines
acceptability
tradeoffs
patron
assumes
responsibility
real
sense
browser
chosen
proposition
examine
collection
sought
constraints
time
approached
sampling
methods
dependence
pointing
summarizing
abilities

Browsing
Searching
documents
present
researcher
adequate
discovering
catalytic
works
Browsing
accomplishing
discovery
consists
wide
spectrum
idiosyncratic
processes
searching
sampling
evaluating
documents
significant
attributes
target
goal
fully
articulated
evident
Serendipity
dumb
luck
willingness
Topic
perception
researchers
variety
fields
serendipity
luck
browsing
process
standing
outside
formal
bibliographical
apparatus
significant
contribution
work

Overhage
Harman
Profiles
scholars
sciences
social
sciences
scholar
search
literature
obviously
relevant
Overhage
Harman
acknowledge
possible
value
unlikely
item
connections
evaluations
need
aware
critical
distinction
roots
agricultural
etymology
browsing
Oxford
English
Dictionary
notes
browse
feed
leaves
shoots
humanities
indicate
researchers
established
access
mechanisms
finding
documents
Olaisen
Webb
importance
ascribed

browsing
shunning
formal
access
methods
demonstrate
awareness
standard
formal
systems
representing
trees
shrubs
crop
shoots
tender
parts
carelessly
used
graze
properly
implying
cropping
scanty
vegetation
entry
grazing
adds
feed
growing
grass
herbage
cattle
feed
pasture
tend
feeding
animal
browsing
hunting
sustenance
find
evaluate
food
animal
grazing
simply
eating
area

supply
evaluation
issues
Browsing
deliberate
searching
scholar
browsing
serious
work
deliberate
search
new
connections
support
new
connections
Browsing
idle
purposeless
undirected
though
clearly
defined
target
topic
grazing
activities
library
data
base
termed
browsing
librarians
related
works
nearby
shelves
supporting
browsing
determining
connections
establish
relatedness
supplying
pasture
tending
user
supporting

grazing
browsing
proposed
scholarly
search
method
anonymous
reviewer
contended
Searching
implies
fairly
conceptualized
query
reviewers
emphasis
mind
Anonymous
thought
articulatea
distinction
grazing
browsing
enable
model
differences
information
access
services
provided
organizations
idiosyncratic
seeking
individual
scholar
articulated
topic
grazing
suffices
mean
results
achieved
differences
descriptive
terms
searcher
system
differences
level

generality
needs
searcher
description
document
translation
reference
librarian
electronic
thesaurus
addition
weighted
query
systems
machine
search
acceptable
document
serve
match
searcher
topic
document
topic
function
filling
knowledge
gap
scholar
specify
topic
fill
gap
browsing
appropriate
term
scholar
set
detective
knowing
problem
area
preconceived
topical
description
way
implies
lack
deliberateness

scholars
query
conceptualized
necessary
tagged
precisely
hampered
inappropriate
satisfaction
derived
illusion
knowledge
Boorstien
noted
walk
reference
librarian
shown
new
knowledge
documents
subject
heading
pointed
known
available
new
Similarly
expect
scholar
topical
description
knowledge
gap
Of
course
scholar
agent
representation
clearly
stated
goal
search
considerations
segmenting
collection
representing
documents
entirely

useless
varying
degrees
articualtion
knowledge
gap
Optimal
searching
levels
articulation
segmenting
collection
assigning
probabilities
utility
question
circumstance
scholar
crop
scanty
vegetation
order
bring
light
undiscovered
public
knowledge
decide
construct
tools
facilitate
scanning
penetrating
evaluating
times
simply
stepping
aside
entirely
best
method
facilitating
representation
evident
scholars
fact
searching
representation
concrete

elements
activity
otimized
explored
information
seeking
behavior
private
investigators
noted
concern
details
variety
levels
specificity
launching
subroutines
synthesis
analysis
simultaneously
detective
model
serves
scholarly
browser
moment
lines
analysis
bserved
patterns
details
eureka
moment
scholar
bears
striking
resemblance
detectives
moment
discovery
case
remain
active
file
maybe
ten
years
middle
different

case
taking
confession
theres
hint
clue
wham
short
circuit
brain
idea
formal
bibliographical
apparatus
entire
set
tools
access
documents
designed
organizations
individuals
individual
searcher
includes
traditional
indexing
abstracting
Library
Congress
classification
subject
headings
Dewey
classification
Boolean
searching
database
utilities
Dialog
bibliographies
footnotes
artificial
intelligence
engines
look
similarities
seed
document

works
collection
selective
dissemination
information
SDI
services
However
documents
collection
represented
clearly
defined
topics
scholars
need
material
resolve
problem
serve
function
represented
topic
set
topics
Wilson
Maron
Robertson
nature
tradeoffs
inherent
representation
documents
bibliographic
apparatus
nature
scholarly
questions
lie
heart
difficulties
scholarly
users
collection
bibliographical
apparatus
determines
subset
attributes

document	Reduction	documents
available	ambiguity	supporting
Figure	compelling	research
likewise	reason	efforts
subset	descriptive	discovery
attributes	cataloging	single
searcher	subject	document
useable	analysis	serves
search	provided	generate
attributes	access	new
document	mechanisms	knowledge
represented	thriving	fill
include	ambiguity	crucial
descriptive	recognized	gap
tags	primary	discovery
author	quality	seed
title	creative	document
date	activity	Blair
publisher	OConnor	Bates
subject	Browsing	packet
descriptors	Response	seed
topics	Subject	documents
determined	Indeterminacy	provide
system	Browsing	fruitful
addressed	animals	pathways
work	engage	collection
attributes	search	Using
scholar	sample	seed
allowed	procedures	documents
descriptive	important	searcher
functional	task	identify
example	maintaining	representation
simple	survival	methods
topic	activity	employed
descriptions	neither	system
question	casual	describe
languages	simply	useful
acceptable	dumb	target
documents	luck	concept
dates	Bell	essentially
publishers	studious	searcher
fundamental	researcher	find
disjunction	browsing	Waltz
purposes	serve	Browsing
formal	significant	provides
bibliographical	tool	scholar
apparatus	discovery	rectify
requirements	useful	situation
scholar	catalytic	overlap

query
concept
articulated
vague
posited
terms
applied
bibliographical
agency
Different
sampling
strategies
engaged
depending
reason
lack
overlap
strategies
browsing
identified
sorts
internal
functional
representation
anomalous
state
knowledge
scholar
bring
collection
distinct
topical
retrieval
typical
bibliographical
apparatus
designed
type
anomalous
state
knowledge
scholar
brings
collection
determine
sampling
evaluation
strategies
play

significant
commonalities
four
sorts
browsing
activity
described
terms
point
collection
browsing
sampling
size
attributes
document
considered
attributes
scholar
sort
comparison
document
scholar
attributes
four
sorts
activity
call
browsing
regions
spectrum
activity
distinct
activities
share
attributes
listed
above
assume
searcher
representation
evaluation
documents
four
sorts
activity
expansion
segmenting
ranking
vague

awarenes
monitoring
information
environment
catalyzing
new
knowledge
shaking
knowledge
store
Expansion
termed
known
topic
search
sense
boundary
case
grazing
browsing
arrangement
documents
shelf
file
closeness
topics
similar
putting
animal
pasture
suitable
document
documents
similarity
attributes
nearby
long
attribute
shelf
position
determined
attribute
sought
scholar
expansion
either
side
useful
results

browsing
activity
begins
targeted
search
degree
nearby
topics
originally
considered
articulated
subsequent
engagement
functional
boundary
topical
functional
grazing
browsing
porous
sampling
locations
specified
location
known
item
known
class
size
sample
limited
studiousness
exists
high
overlap
query
attribute
list
document
attribute
list
Moving
original
target
document
present
data
attributes
ways

characterizing
attributes
previously
overlooked
necessarily
case
movement
known
item
result
less
overlap
doc
query
result
modification
query
Vague
awareness
searches
conducted
searcher
aware
problem
lack
state
concisely
exactly
though
useful
document
recognized
glimpsed
searcher
makes
formal
bibliographic
apparatus
order
partitioning
collection
ranked
probabilities
utility
primary
concept
maximize
amount
useful

data
takes
analysis
Suppose
notice
frequent
similar
metaphors
news
reports
illness
begin
wonder
mythology
illness
social
consequences
representation
disease
feminine
virtue
consumption
relates
AIDS
funding
dealing
representation
illness
curiosity
ways
disease
beyond
assault
infectious
agent
biological
process
gone
awry
look
Library
Congress
Subject
Headings
list
Representation
Disease
find
heading

key
word
search
using
disease
representation
work
Disease
Representation
Images
Illness
Madness
AIDS
References
work
prove
interesting
though
Library
Congress
Subject
Headings
applied
Mental
illness
History
Diseases
art
Disease
Psychology
Medicine
Art
Sick
role
mention
art
prove
useful
though
works
listed
relevance
recall
Susan
Sontag
written
illness
metaphor
author

search
turn
AIDS
Metaphors
interesting
references
happen
work
Lakeoff
find
insights
individual
social
representation
though
obvious
connection
societal
representation
disease
subject
headings
Categorization
Psychology
Cognition
Thought
Thinking
work
labeled
immediately
think
looking
Women
Art
N
Fine
Arts
section
collection
work
title
obviously
relevant
Idols
Perversity
chapter
entitled
Cult
Invalidism

chapter
examines
role
painting
exploiting
romanticizing
notion
woman
permanent
necessary
natural
invalid
image
second
half
nineteenth
century
control
infrequently
destroy
lives
countless
European
American
women
associated
references
considerable
interest
possible
characterize
knowledge
gap
giving
examples
possible
areas
items
interest
single
small
set
topical
descriptors
search
specific
sampling
location
broad

segmenting
collection
zones
less
prove
fruitful
ranking
sample
size
though
size
small
maximize
number
glimpses
time
unit
Morse
relaxed
specification
threshold
overlap
query
attributes
document
attributes
Monitoring
information
environment
rests
assumption
individual
scholar
heshe
know
everything
individual
discipline
clearly
articulated
query
sampling
methods
keep
scholar
aware
new
developments
place

mean
skimming
tables
contents
scanning
shelves
portions
collection
new
titles
chatting
colleagues
Location
size
sample
preset
based
satisfactory
level
overlap
attribute
lists
previous
experience
region
high
variability
attribute
values
new
acquisitions
section
new
nonfiction
sampling
mechanism
set
mechanisms
constrained
set
attributes
generalized
appropriate
language
reading
ability
fields
cognate
interests

searcher
specific
attributes
search
time
simple
implementation
approach
common
acquisitions
collection
new
book
section
Herein
small
number
documents
date
present
classified
order
random
order
subset
collection
documents
fields
breadth
collection
Any
document
seems
interesting
contain
references
descriptors
leading
collection
Time
condensed
novelty
high
Catalyzing
new
knowledge
creativity
ability
combinations

dichotomous
previously
unrelated
concepts
evaluate
combination
possible
fit
accommodating
model
Rothenberg
Browsing
enables
combining
user-selected
characteristics
searcher
user-selected
set
characteristics
document
evaluating
utility
combination
intent
generate
new
combination
way
segment
collection
Short
engaging
document
random
sampling
assumption
location
fruitful
results
approach
browsing
assumes
extremely
relaxed
threshold
congruence
scholar
attributes

document
attributes
prespecification
prediction
useful
class
individual
entity
attributes
useful
negative
specification
NOT
documents
classes
familiar
specification
search
query
attributes
limiting
case
know
dont
know
need
know
entertain
combination
attributes
neither
sampling
location
sampling
size
degree
congruence
attribute
lists
specified
Informal
discussions
faculty
members
working
research
libraries
provided
variations

search
strategy
park
car
write
license
number
nearby
car
Go
section
shelves
call
numbers
documents
contain
numbers
license
plate
sampling
Expect
time
search
nothing
spark
ignite
new
idea
Components
Browsing
Activity
Having
looked
four
sorts
browsing
activity
examine
primary
components
activities
sense
subgoals
achieved
steps
attributes
discussed
above
subgoals

components
useful
labels
glimpses
connect
attributes
evaluate
connection
evaluate
search
Browsing
approaches
difficulties
posed
subject
indeterminacy
removing
constraints
content
size
attribute
lists
searcher
document
scholar
engage
attribute
set
attributes
matter
unrelated
seem
topic
Hobby
interests
title
undergraduate
course
cognitive
style
political
leanings
color
preferences
self
descriptors
ranging
trivial
substantial

engaged
ad
hoc
way
search
goes
functional
requirements
stimulating
search
guide
choice
starting
point
sampling
point
evaluation
criteria
Similarly
studiousness
searcher
determine
sampling
size
search
evaluation
number
iterations
process
physical
nature
collection
collection
hard
copy
documents
full
text
database
database
representations
manner
glimpses
locations
glimpses
phase
process
discovering
difference

makes
difference
Bateson
examination
document
attributes
order
evaluate
documents
potential
resolving
anomalous
state
knowledge
Belkin
searcher
read
engage
term
documents
media
coding
subset
coding
comprehensible
representation
coding
Morse
proposed
maximizing
likelihood
discovery
maximizing
number
glimpses
time
unit
Morse
glimpse
inputing
document
attribute
searchers
connection
making
system
Selection
starting
point

collection
identification
sector
searched
amounts
global
glimpse
megadocument
comprised
collection
importance
selection
manner
selection
dependent
type
question
initiating
response
searcher
vague
idea
useful
document
useful
select
portions
collection
connection
concept
searcher
seeking
shake
knowledge
store
Overhage
Harman
effort
generate
sustain
creative
activity
random
starting
point
engaged
though
entirely
random

portion
collection
searcher
familiar
left
search
Examination
attributes
individual
documents
glimpsing
local
level
searcher
minimize
time
useful
glimpses
inhibiting
ability
evaluate
attribute
evident
individual
glimpse
individual
glimpse
instrument
enables
searcher
create
appropriate
representation
system
representation
set
rules
elements
document
selected
highlighted
browsing
searcher
rule
maker
searcher
vary
rules
input

lack
input
warrants
useful
value
attribute
sort
attribute
determined
ad
hoc
scholar
interacting
collection
Control
depth
penetration
collection
identified
Intrex
study
primary
attribute
browsing
Overhage
Harman
collection
documents
effect
stream
data
incidently
segmented
books
videos
database
records
searcher
start
point
virtual
stream
documents
move
points
making
glimpses
physical
conceptual

chunks
data
collection
example
classification
segments
series
individual
documents
point
stream
user
penetrate
collection
depth
chapter
verse
sentence
phrase
example
Figure
Any
datum
depth
related
datum
depth
point
stream
depth
point
stream
control
enables
searcher
represent
document
useful
level
specificity
point
document
glimpses
input
data
directly
document
issue
translation

differing
terms
concept
happens
external
representation
document
certainty
searcher
discover
useful
concept
work
hand
addresses
sample
size
number
document
data
items
considered
glimpse
wrong
size
catch
emphasize
contents
address
issue
searcher
vocabulary
expertise
decode
text
appropriately
new
knowledge
sought
relevant
concept
recognizable
connect
attributes
Central
creative
activity
gullibility
willingness

catch
similarities
OConnor
holding
antithetical
propositions
requires
searcher
know
thyself
available
full
array
appropriate
attributes
current
values
internal
representation
type
search
determine
attributes
value
vague
awareness
knowledge
gap
driving
search
titles
subtitles
limited
set
subject
areas
appropriate
search
driven
desire
generate
new
knowledge
impossible
predict
attribute
attribute
value
meaningful

searcher
look
document
attributes
sort
size
level
specificity
Single
words
entire
chapters
analogs
media
style
level
presumed
expertise
type
graphics
authorial
stance
color
binding
location
collection
physical
attributes
conceptual
attributes
considered
searcher
document
set
documents
comprise
answer
share
significant
set
attributes
description
searcher
Search
query
attributes
browsing
range
limited

set
qualities
unspecified
volatile
set
sense
play
point
vary
document
attributes
compared
sampling
mechanism
Three
sorts
connections
document
attributes
searcher
attributes
possible
document
attribute
paired
searcher
attribute
evaluation
valid
proposition
document
attribute
link
act
catalyst
linking
attributes
searchers
internal
representation
problem
Similarly
internal
representation
attribute
link
serve
catalyst
linking

document
attributes
Achieving
threshold
degree
overlap
document
attributes
searcher
attributes
tantamount
putting
search
query
document
description
probabilistic
classification
Of
course
determination
constitutes
significant
overlap
remains
searcher
attribute
sufficient
threshold
percentage
required
either
general
characteristics
class
document
attributes
congruent
query
attributes
used
fill
scholars
knowledge
gap
refine
search
process
evaluate

connection
Just
browsing
transfers
representation
documents
queries
searcher
transfers
responsibilities
evaluation
documents
bibliographical
apparatus
evaluation
statement
match
significant
overlap
topic
descriptors
questions
topic
descriptors
documents
reduces
burden
analysis
searcher
presents
difficulties
failures
subject
indeterminacy
Conversation
hemispheres
Kaminuma
human
information
processing
paradigms
brings
pattern
recognition
capabilities
right
logicosymbolic
capabilities
left

idiosyncratic
search
combinations
attributes
generated
glimpsed
data
subjected
testing
scrutiny
searchers
evaluative
abilities
Figure
paraphrase
Pauling
way
ideas
generate
lot
connections
simply
throw
bad
OConnor
Of
course
simply
throwing
bad
entirely
selfevident
bear
resemblance
formal
methodologies
relevant
discipline
though
evaluations
total
disregard
methods
case
momentary
validity
linkage
proposition
rest

pattern
right
hemisphere
evaluation
logical
analysis
linkage
prove
valid
show
way
evaluative
conversation
gullibility
presupposes
considerable
studiousness
senses
First
time
allocated
immersion
topic
set
topics
immersion
undergirds
recognition
patterns
facility
methodology
normally
associated
expertise
Second
time
ability
applied
individual
search
considerable
though
course
possibility
useful
item
search
possible
evaluate

search
Linked
closely
connection
evaluation
evaluation
search
outcome
connection
evaluation
satisfactory
connection
nota
satisfactory
connection
decision
connection
judged
satisfactory
need
mean
hold
further
scrutiny
seems
worth
pursuing
search
considered
complete
browsing
continue
considered
second
search
scholar
looking
new
connections
nature
search
change
scholar
looks
supportive
materials
connection
judged
satisfactory

decision
search
sufficient
resources
time
enthusiasm
money
continue
searching
time
search
continued
decision
local
level
sampling
continue
level
attribute
sample
location
change
absence
clearly
articulated
target
suggests
determining
search
finished
Discovery
useful
document
suggest
end
search
suggest
line
continued
search
Exhaustion
resources
bring
halt
current
search
process
need
considered

failed
search
portions
collection
examined
time
need
considered
next
time
course
discovery
subsequent
search
triggers
connection
previously
examined
document
personal
nature
searching
literature
obviously
relevant
Overhage
Harman
necessarily
render
bibliographical
institution
helpless
System
resources
devoted
enabling
rapid
presentation
attributes
rapid
informed
evaluation
connections
Key
word
searching
rapid
scanning
long

lists	imposed	stacks
hits	book	works
Internet	covers	discussion
surfing	database	idiosyncratic
library	files	nature
seconds	consequence	browsing
speak	long	activities
capability	useful	makes
system	information	observation
resources	Computers	analysis
shrink	serve	browsers
time	store	difficult
required	weighted	best
examine	topical	possible
document	descriptors	questions
attributes	nontopical	goals
Mechanisms	evaluative	results
abstract	descriptors	measurements
construction	documents	physical
enable	Blair	attributes
system	OConnor	location
facilitate	characterize	time
idiosyncratic	documents	imagine
browsing	browsers	tracking
activity	useful	eye
Abstract	ways	movements
defined	Adding	timing
smaller	user	searchers
quantity	profiles	engagement
containing	adds	individual
virtue	possibility	elements
power	looking	documents
Simpson	documents	significant
abstract	useful	difficulties
enables	type	remain
searcher	previous	determining
decision	searcher	criteria
expending	discipline	used
less	position	select
effort	affiliation	document
required	optional	appropriate
engage	functions	equally
document	video	meaningful
document	game	why
collection	flight	attributes
document	simulator	engaged
scholar	bring	why
concerned	delight	documents
boundaries	walking	overlooked

Browsing
powerful
tool
discovery
valuable
mass
mostly
worthless
uninteresting
Wilson
documents
Browsing
activity
offers

probe
valued
scholars
precisely
operates
outside
bounds
formal
access
system
Therefore
provides
window
view

expanded
concepts
representation
concepts
chapter
appeared
Browsing
Framework
Seeking
Functional
Information
Knowledge
December

Table 8.2
Extracted Words from Table 8.1 Alphabetized with Frequencies

AIDS	3	Fine	1	Perversity	1
Abstract	1	First	1	Profiles	1
Achieving	1	Framework	1	Psychology	2
Activity	1	Functional	1	Reduction	1
Adding	1	Go	1	References	1
American	1	Harman	5	Representa	3
Anonymous	1	Headings	2	Response	1
Any	2	Herein	1	Robertson	1
Art	2	History	1	Rothenberg	1
Arts	1	Hobby	1	SDI	1
Bates	1	However	2	Search	1
Bateson	1	Idols	1	Searching	2
Belkin	1	Illness	1	Second	1
Bell	1	Images	1	Seeking	1
Blair	2	Indetermin	1	Selection	2
Blairs	1	Informal	1	Serendipit	1
Boolean	1	Informatio	1	Short	1
Boorstien	1	Internet	1	Sick	1
Browsing	13	Intrex	1	Similarly	3
Catalyzing	1	Invalidism	1	Simpson	1
Categoriza	1	Just	1	Single	1
Clearly	1	Kaminuma	1	Sontag	1
Cognition	1	Key	1	Subject	3
Components	1	Knowledge	1	Subsequent	1
Computers	1	Lakeoff	1	Suppose	1
Congress	3	Library	3	Susan	1
Control	1	Linked	1	Swanson	1
Conversati	1	Location	1	System	1
Cult	1	Madness	1	Therefore	1
December	1	Maron	1	Thinking	1
Dewey	1	Mechanisms	1	Thought	1
Dialog	1	Medicine	1	Three	1
Dictionary	1	Mental	1	Time	1
Different	1	Metaphors	1	Topic	1
Discovery	1	Monitoring	1	Using	1
Disease	3	Morse	3	Vague	1
Diseases	1	Moving	1	Waltz	1
Earlier	1	N	1	Webb	1
English	1	NOT	1	Wilson	2
European	1	OConnor	5	Women	1
Examinatio	1	Of	3	abilities	2
Exhaustion	1	Optimal	1	ability	5
Expansion	1	Olaisen	1	above	2
Expect	1	Overhage	5	absence	1
Farrow	1	Oxford	1	abstract	2
Figure	3	Pauling	1	abstractin	3

acceptabil	1	art	2	bserved	1
acceptable	2	articualti	1	burden	1
access	7	articulate	9	call	2
accommodat	1	articulati	1	capabiliti	2
accomplish	2	artificial	1	capability	1
achieved	2	ascribed	1	capable	1
acknowledg	1	aside	1	car	2
acquisitio	2	assault	1	carelessly	1
act	1	assigning	1	case	6
active	1	associated	2	casual	1
activities	4	assume	1	cataloging	1
activity	13	assumes	2	catalyst	2
ad	3	assumption	2	catalytic	2
addition	1	attribute	22	catch	2
address	1	attributes	49	cattle	1
addressed	1	author	2	century	1
addresses	1	authorial	1	certainty	1
adds	2	available	3	change	1
adequate	1	aware	3	change	1
affiliatio	1	awareness	3	chapter	4
agency	1	awarenessm	1	chapters	1
agent	3	awry	1	characteri	6
agricultur	1	bad	2	chatting	1
allocated	1	base	1	choice	1
allowed	1	based	1	chosen	1
ambiguity	2	bear	1	chunks	1
amount	1	bears	1	circuit	1
amounts	1	begin	1	circumstan	1
analogs	1	begins	1	class	3
analysis	7	behavior	1	classes	1
animal	3	best	3	classifica	4
animals	1	beyond	1	classified	1
anomalous	3	bibliograp	11	clearly	5
anonymous	1	binding	1	closely	1
answer	1	biological	1	closeness	1
antithetic	1	book	2	clue	1
apparatus	8	books	1	coding	4
appeared	1	boundaries	1	cognate	1
applied	3	boundary	2	cognitive	1
approach	2	bounds	1	colleagues	1
approached	1	brain	1	collection	36
approaches	2	breadth	1	color	2
appropriat	7	bring	4	combinatio	6
aproblem	1	brings	2	combining	1
area	2	broad	1	common	1
areas	2	browse	1	commonalit	1
areexpansi	1	browser	2	compared	1
arrangemen	1	browsers	2	comparison	1
array	1	browsing	29	compelling	1

complete	1	creativity	1	different	1
complicate	1	criteria	2	differing	1
components	2	critical	1	difficult	1
comprehens	1	criticized	1	difficulti	4
comprise	1	crop	2	directly	1
comprised	1	cropping	1	discipline	3
concept	8	crucial	1	discover	1
concepts	3	curiosity	1	discoverin	2
conceptual	3	current	2	discovery	7
concern	1	data	8	discoveryA	1
concerned	1	database	5	discussed	3
concisely	1	date	2	discussion	3
concrete	1	dates	1	disease	4
condensed	1	datum	2	disjunctio	1
conducted	1	dealing	1	disregard	1
confession	1	decide	1	disseminat	1
congruence	2	decision	5	distinct	2
congruent	1	decode	1	distinctio	2
connect	1	defined	3	doc	1
connection	20	degree	3	document	47
consequenc	2	degrees	1	documents	38
considerab	3	deliberate	3	dont	1
considerat	1	delight	1	driven	1
considered	8	demonstrat	1	driving	1
consists	1	dependence	1	dumb	2
constitute	1	dependent	1	eating	1
constraine	1	depending	1	effect	1
constraint	2	depth	7	effort	3
construct	1	derived	1	efforts	1
constructi	1	describe	1	either	2
constructs	1	described	1	electronic	1
consumptio	1	descriptio	6	elements	3
contain	2	descriptiv	4	emphasis	1
containing	1	descriptor	8	emphasize	1
contended	1	designed	2	employed	1
content	1	desire	1	enable	2
contents	2	destroy	1	enables	4
continue	3	details	2	enabling	1
continued	2	detective	2	end	1
contributi	1	detectives	1	engage	4
control	3	determinat	1	engaged	5
conversati	1	determine	3	engaged	1
copy	1	determined	3	engagement	3
countless	1	determines	2	engaging	1
course	6	determinin	3	engines	1
covers	1	developmen	1	enhancing	1
create	1	devoted	1	entertain	1
creation	1	dichotomou	1	enthusiasm	1
creative	4	difference	5	entire	2

entirely	4	feeding	1	graze	1
entitled	1	feminine	1	grazing	8
entity	1	fields	3	growing	1
entry	1	file	2	guide	1
environmen	2	files	1	gullibilit	2
equally	1	fill	3	half	1
essential	1	filling	1	halt	1
essentiall	1	find	4	hampered	1
establish	1	finding	1	hand	1
establishe	1	finished	1	happen	1
etymology	1	fit	1	happens	1
eureka	1	flight	1	hard	1
evaluate	6	food	1	heading	2
evaluating	3	footnotes	1	headings	2
evaluation	15	form	1	heart	1
evaluative	3	formal	8	helpless	1
everything	1	formulates	1	hemisphere	2
evident	3	four	4	herbage	1
exactly	1	frequent	1	heshe	1
examinatio	1	fruitful	3	high	3
examine	3	full	2	highlighte	1
examined	3	fully	1	highlighti	1
examines	1	function	2	hint	1
example	3	functional	6	hits	1
examples	1	functions	1	hoc	3
exists	1	fundamenta	2	hold	1
expanded	1	funding	1	holding	1
expansion	1	further	2	human	1
expect	1	game	1	humanities	1
expending	1	gap	8	hunting	1
experience	1	general	1	idea	3
expertise	3	generality	1	ideas	1
exploiting	1	generalize	1	identifica	1
exploratio	1	generate	5	identified	2
explored	1	generated	1	identify	1
external	2	getting	1	idiosyncra	5
extremely	1	giving	1	idle	1
eye	1	glimpse	5	ignite	1
facilitate	2	glimpsed	2	illness	5
facilitati	1	glimpses	7	illusion	1
facility	1	glimpsesco	1	image	1
fact	1	glimpsing	1	imagine	1
faculty	1	global	1	immediatel	1
failed	1	goal	2	immersion	2
failure	2	goals	1	implementa	1
failures	1	goes	1	implies	2
fairly	1	gone	1	implying	1
familiar	2	graphics	1	importance	2
feed	3	grass	1	important	1

imposed	1	lack	3	maintainin	1
impossible	1	language	1	maker	1
improved	1	languages	1	makes	3
inappropri	1	launching	1	making	2
incidently	1	leading	1	manner	2
include	1	leanings	1	mass	1
includes	1	leaves	3	match	2
incomplete	1	left	2	material	1
indetermin	4	less	3	materials	1
indexing	3	level	8	matter	1
indicate	1	levels	2	maximize	2
individual	14	librarian	2	maximizing	2
indiviual	1	librarians	1	maybe	1
infectious	1	libraries	1	mean	3
informatio	8	library	2	meaningful	2
informed	1	license	2	measuremen	1
infrequent	1	lie	1	mechanism	2
inherent	1	light	1	mechanisms	3
inhibiting	1	likelihood	3	media	2
initiating	1	likewise	1	megadocume	1
input	3	limited	3	mention	1
inputing	1	limiting	1	members	1
insights	1	line	1	metaphors	1
institutio	1	lines	1	metaphor	1
instrument	1	link	2	method	4
intelligen	1	linkage	2	methodolog	2
intent	1	linking	1	methods	6
interactin	1	list	1	middle	1
interactio	1	linking	1	mind	1
interest	2	list	2	minimize	1
interestin	3	listed	1	model	3
interests	2	lists	1	moderate	1
internal	4	listed	1	modificati	1
invalid	1	lists	3	moment	3
investigat	1	literature	2	momentary	1
issue	2	lives	1	money	1
issues	1	local	2	mostly	1
item	4	location	8	move	1
items	2	locations	2	movement	1
iterations	1	logical	1	movements	1
judged	2	logicosymb	1	mythology	1
keep	1	long	3	natural	1
key	1	look	3	nature	6
know	5	looked	1	nearby	4
knowing	1	looking	3	necessaril	2
knowledge	21	looks	1	necessary	2
known	5	lot	1	need	6
labeled	1	luck	3	needs	1
labels	1	machine	1	negative	1

neither	2	penetrate	1	probabilit	2
new	18	penetratin	1	probe	1
news	1	penetratio	2	problem	4
next	1	percentage	6	problems	1
nineteenth	1	perception	1	procedures	1
nonfiction	1	permanent	1	proceedure	1
nontopical	1	personal	1	process	7
normally	1	phase	1	processes	1
nota	1	phrase	1	processing	1
noted	2	physical	4	profiles	1
notes	1	picture	1	properly	1
notesThe	1	place	2	proposed	2
nothing	1	plate	1	propositio	3
notice	1	play	2	prove	1
notion	1	point	11	propositio	1
novelty	1	pointed	1	prove	3
number	6	pointing	1	provide	1
numbers	2	points	1	provided	3
observatio	1	political	1	provides	2
obvious	1	porous	1	public	2
obviously	3	portion	1	publisher	1
offers	1	portions	3	publishers	1
operates	1	posed	1	purposeles	1
option	1	posited	1	purposes	1
optional	1	position	2	pursuing	1
order	5	possibilit	2	putting	2
organizati	2	possible	7	qualities	1
original	1	potential	2	quality	1
originally	1	power	1	quantity	1
otimizedWe	1	powerful	1	queries	1
outcome	1	precisely	2	query	13
outside	2	preconceiv	1	question	3
overlap	9	predict	1	questions	4
overlooked	2	prediction	1	random	4
packet	1	preference	1	range	1
painting	1	present	3	ranging	1
paired	1	presentati	1	ranked	1
paradigms	1	presented	1	ranking	2
paraphrase	1	presents	1	rapid	3
park	1	preset	1	read	1
partitioni	1	prespecifi	1	reading	1
parts	1	presumed	1	real	1
party	1	presuppose	1	reason	2
pasture	3	previous	2	recall	1
pathways	1	previously	3	recognitio	2
patron	9	primary	4	recognizab	1
patrons	2	priori	1	recognized	2
pattern	2	private	1	records	1
patterns	2	probabilis	1	rectify	1

reduces	1	satisfacto	5	shelves	3
reference	2	scanning	3	shoots	2
references	3	scanty	2	short	1
refine	1	scholar	25	shortcomin	1
region	1	scholarly	5	show	1
regions	1	scholars	7	shown	1
related	2	sciences	2	shrink	1
relatednes	1	scientific	1	shrubs	1
relates	1	scrutiny	2	shunning	1
relaxed	2	search	43	side	1
relevance	1	search	1	significan	9
relevant	6	searched	1	similar	2
remain	2	searcher	38	similariti	2
remains	1	searchers	4	similarity	1
removing	1	searches	1	simple	2
render	1	searching	9	simply	5
reports	1	second	2	simulator	1
represent	1	seconds	1	simultaneo	1
representa	24	section	4	single	2
represente	4	seed	1	situation	1
representi	2	sector	1	size	10
required	3	seed	3	sizewhich	1
requiremen	3	seeking	3	skimming	1
requires	2	seem	1	small	4
research	2	seems	2	smaller	1
researcher	4	segment	1	social	3
resemblanc	2	segmented	1	societal	1
resolve	1	segmenting	3	sort	2
resolving	1	segments	1	sorts	6
resources	5	select	2	sought	3
response	2	selected	1	spark	1
responsibi	2	selection	2	speak	1
rest	1	selective	1	speaking	1
rests	1	self	1	specific	2
result	2	selfeviden	1	specificat	3
results	4	sense	4	specificit	3
retrieval	2	senses	1	specified	2
retrieving	1	sentence	1	specify	1
reviewer	1	serendipit	1	spectrum	2
reviewers	1	series	1	stacks	1
right	2	serious	1	stance	1
role	2	serve	5	standard	1
romanticiz	1	serves	2	standing	1
roots	1	services	2	start	1
rule	1	set	17	starting	3
rules	3	shake	1	starts	1
sample	6	shaking	1	state	4
sampling	16	share	2	stated	1
satisfacti	1	shelf	2	statement	1

stepping	1	tender	1	unrelated	1
steps	1	tending	1	unlikely	1
stimulatin	1	term	2	unrelated	1
store	3	termed	2	unspecifie	1
strategies	3	terms	5	useable	1
strategy	1	testing	1	used	3
stream	5	text	2	useful	20
striking	2	theory	2	useless	1
studious	1	theres	1	user	3
studiousne	3	thesaurus	1	users	1
study	1	think	1	user-select	2
style	2	though	9	using	1
subgoals	2	thought	1	utilities	1
subject	10	threshold	4	utility	3
subjected	1	thriving	1	vague	4
subroutine	1	throw	1	valid	2
subsequent	2	throwing	1	validity	1
subset	4	thyself	1	valuable	1
substantia	1	time	15	value	4
subtitles	1	times	1	valued	1
suffices	1	timing	1	values	2
sufficient	2	title	3	variabilit	1
suggest	2	titles	2	variations	1
suggests	1	tool	2	variety	2
suitable	1	tools	2	vary	2
summarizin	1	topic	12	varying	1
supply	1	topical	6	vegetation	2
supplying	1	topics	7	verified	1
support	1	total	1	verse	1
supporting	3	tracking	1	video	1
supportive	1	tradeoff	1	videos	1
surfing	1	tradeoffs	2	view	1
survival	1	traditiona	1	virtual	1
sustain	1	transfers	2	virtue	2
sustenance	1	translatio	2	vocabulary	1
synthesis	1	trees	1	volatile	1
system	10	triggers	1	walk	1
systems	2	trivial	1	walking	1
tables	1	troubling	1	warrants	1
tagged	1	turn	1	way	5
tags	1	type	5	ways	3
takes	2	typical	1	weighted	2
taking	1	undergirds	1	well	1
tantamount	1	undergradu	1	wham	1
target	5	undirected	1	why	2
targeted	1	undiscover	2	wide	1
task	1	uninterest	1	willingnes	2
ten	1	unit	2	window	1
tend	1	unknowabil	1	woman	1

women	1	working	1	written	1
wonder	1	works	5	wrong	1
word	2	worth	1	years	1
words	1	worthless	1	zones	1
work	10	write	1		

Chapter 9
Aboutness and User-Generated Descriptors

The images in figure 9.1, together with their accompanying descriptions, point to a major problem in the representation of documents. Different users may well have very different notions of what the document is *about*.[1] This highlights the access problem for users who must depend on the judgment and coding of someone else.

Background

Two case studies of uses of photographs provide a different avenue of approach to the representation of documents. The first case involves a chance discovery of some antique lantern-slide images; the second is based on PhotoCD technology. The two cases span the use of photographs in educational environments from the late nineteenth century to the present, and they both point toward an enriched mode of representation.

During the renovation of the administration building at a small university on the Great Plains, several small wooden boxes were discovered in the clutter. A few were salvaged because of their attractive appearance. One faculty member noticed that each box contained glass lantern slides and attempted to save as many boxes as possible. Approximately 15 boxes were eventually located. Each box contained approximately 100 slides.

Each slide is a sandwich of two sheets of glass (.0625 inches x 4 inches x 3.25 inches); a piece of roll film (typically, but not always, 2.25 inches x 3 inches); masking material of various sorts; and tape bindings. The physical condition of the slides varies from excellent to poor. Many show no signs of wear or damage, whereas others have cracks in the glass or problems with mold growth. The subject matter of the necessarily haphazard sample of slides ranges widely. A partial list of the topic areas includes:

- Hand-tinted copies of engravings of the *Aeneid*

- Portraits of writers and artists—Renaissance to late nineteenth century

- Locales mentioned in literary works

- old man
- 19th-century clothes
- Walt Whitman
- Santa on vacation
- caricature
- nice beard
- casual strength
- serene

- exam week
- Laacoon
- some Greek story
- frustration
- tangled up
- torsion
- stressed out
- agony

- 19th-century beauty
- coziness
- royalty
- antique costume
- fancy woolen wear
- stern
- exploitive royalty
- pretty

Fig. 9.1. Variety of concept and level of specificity in the description of antique lantern slides.

- Travelogue images of Scotland
- Paintings of classical mythology images
- Statues and other remains from antiquity
- American geography

After these boxes of antique slides were rescued from the brink of destruction, they sat unattended for several months, serving mostly as conversation pieces and paperweights. On occasion a faculty member would think of a way to use some of the images in teaching or research; some of the images were unavailable from more standard sources. However, because no projection facilities were available on the campus for such slides, use was limited and interest did not turn to action.

By chance, a few of the lantern slides were brought to the room where a project on digital analysis of video images was under way. The addition of a home video camera to the computer imaging system enabled input of digitized images of approximately 20 of the lantern-slide images.

On a casual, ad hoc basis, various faculty members and graduate students called up the images on the computer and were uniformly pleased with the results. Several uses for the images in different courses and departments were conceived. Some of these included:

- Source for stage settings and costuming
- Lecture illustrations in history, classics, art history, English
- Source for image fragments in video on collapse of Rome
- Background images in desktop publishing
- Comparison of artifacts with paintings of classical scenes
- Hypermedia stacks for study of Shakespeare and antiquity

As individuals from various disciplines made comments and suggestions, they also began to realize the need for some access system. Several also pointed out that a list of descriptors suitable for people in widely differing fields would have to be long and multifaceted. The stage dresser seeking an image of Hawthorne's home would be looking for different aspects than would an English literature student or a professor of architecture. The vocabulary of these differing users would also be quite different.

Aboutness

Aboutness is the term we use to distinguish functional representation from mere description or application of a topic. We can say that aboutness is extra-descriptive. It is likely to be generated, at least in part, by the subject of a work, though a secondary element to one user may be a primary element to another. Yet it goes beyond that to include "what this means to me." Aboutness is the behavioral reaction of a person to a document. Each patron may have a different experience with the same document. All of the elements we discussed earlier come into play in the personal reaction to the subject elements. We might say that aboutness has an adjectival component, in addition to the noun.

We can imagine the patron looking for "something cheery for springtime," or "something depicting passionate commitment," or "some images showing harmony," or "something that makes me feel good." We may say, then, that aboutness is, indeed, descriptive. It describes the relationship between a user's knowledge state and the physically present document.

Movie critics provide a good example of aboutness judgments. When some critics rave and others pan, it is not because they have seen different physical texts; rather, all the technical knowledge, topical knowledge, emotions, and beliefs of each critic are being engaged in the construction of a reaction to the physical text. Viewers may come to realize that their own complement of knowledge, belief, and emotion structures more closely resemble those of one reviewer than others, so the reviews of that critic will become surrogate aboutness judgments for the user.

Why Photographs?

Photographic images are not words. Photographs are usually very specific representations made at particular moments of particular objects. Words are general representations. Pictures are made more general by adding more pictures in a sequence or collage. Words are made more specific by grouping them with other words. Figure 9.2 illustrates this point.

(General)

CAT

(specific)

Fig. 9.2. Words and pictures; generality and specificity. My young cat, Willie, was photographed behind a toy horse in El Sobrante, California, in October.

We can say that photographs help to make document representation issues more obvious because of the very different ways in which pictures and words work. Word texts can be described with elements directly from the document and similar to daily speech acts. Thus, the possibility for confusion of elements with topic and topic with aboutness runs high.

Likewise, word texts have clearly segmented elements set within rule-bound structures. We can, for example, say that a particular word is a noun and that, because of its place and the places of other words, that noun is the subject of a sentence. At one level, then, we can determine the topical characteristics of a text with some ease and surety. There are, of course, many caveats to such an approach. The meaning of a text for any particular user is heavily dependent on that user. This has been a central theme of our explorations.

Image texts are not constructed in a manner that allows easy demarcation of elements or rules for extraction of *a* subject. Photographs are, in a sense, made by sampling a very broad-band stream of data. They are analog representations with very fine gradations from light to dark. They present no easily discerned noun/verb analogs. There is no rule for translation of a whole image or any of its parts into words.[2] The old phrase "one picture is worth a thousand words" speaks well to the high bandwidth of communication that is possible with image texts. However, there is no saying just how many words or just which words are required to describe any individual picture. A word document has easily discernable units and clusters of units of meaning. Photographs do not.

Human brains are uniquely suited to processing visual information. Nearly 50 percent of the neocortex, the "higher" primate portion of the brain, is devoted to visual processing.[3] We seem to be very good at pattern recognition. So, when we say that pictures cannot easily be translated into words, there is no implication of inferiority of images as a representation medium. As multimedia systems burgeon in many fields, the issues of image representation become more complicated and more compelling.

Pictures represent the object/event space in a manner fundamentally different from words.[4] In turn, representing pictures with words is a vexing challenge. Yet, people do in fact represent pictures with words. If you ask someone what a picture is about, they can usually say something. Reactions to the lantern slides indicated that the "something" is often not just (or even) the object or set of objects in the image. Variety of potential usage generates a variety of conceptual descriptions. Choice among synonymous terms and level of specificity are not the only issues.

Representation of images by words becomes even more problematic when we consider the issue of generalization. The words *horse, elephant,* and *sheep* can be generalized to "animals." We have verbal representations of taxonomic relations. What, though, would we do with a photograph of a horse, a photograph of an elephant, and a photograph of sheep, as we have in figure 9.3? Is it adequate to simply combine all the photographs into a collage? Are combined pictures really a better solution for some circumstances, as the word *animals* could include many things besides the horse, elephant, and sheep?

boy and horse

elephant

sheep

Fig. 9.3. Three Photographs. Individual pictures can be viewed separately or together, but there is no way to combine them into a single image that produces a generalization equivalent to the verbal: Horse, elephant, and sheep > animals.

Subject indeterminacy causes search failures within the realm of word-based documents, in which both the documents and the representations are words. How, then, are we to represent photographs with words and expect successful searches? Aboutness presents a challenge to which we have already alluded. If we have a difficult time avoiding indeterminacy in word representations of word documents, how can we possibly expand the number of conceptual tags with image-based documents? Although images have been in use for millenia, only recently has any large percentage of the population had the ability to make and use images. This complicates our question because there is no strong, accessible background of visual literacy on which to construct picture-based representations.

In this phase of our explorations of representation, we will continue to use the digital environment. However, we now abandon use of the machine to describe points of change in the physical text. Instead, we examine the possibility of the machine environment making it possible for members of the user group to generate their own descriptors. This engages the users in construction of representations at a different point in the process of representation.

Community Memory Interface

A word-based system for describing the aboutness of pictures can be constructed by changing our model of *where* the act of representation takes place. We have said that typically the rules for representation are established by the external agency. What if we were to reestablish the point of activity as the patron group?

The digital environment enables keeping track of large amounts of data. The storage and manipulation capabilities of a computer could substitute gathering and ranking user-generated descriptors for the typical mere storage of agency-generated descriptors. Such an approach offers potential for:

- Accumulation of as many descriptors as users thought appropriate
- Accommodation of multiple functional concepts
- Accommodation of multiple levels of specificity
- Multiple terms for the same object or concept
- User-determined descriptive terms
- Multiple formats of descriptive terms

There are, of course, also challenges:

- Elicitation of adjectival, functional descriptors
- Adaptation of users to a system that becomes more descriptive over time
- Management of large descriptor lists for popular images

A community memory interface to a collection makes several assumptions. It assumes a new relationship between the interface and the users of the system. The users will be contributing to the system, in a sense customizing it, nurturing it, and teaching it. To illustrate this idea, imagine a recent graduate with a degree in library science beginning work at a reference desk. The new reference librarian, the interface to the collection, knows the documents, but is a blank slate regarding patrons. However, after a time, as clients come into the collection and ask questions, make their likes and dislikes known, and discuss their areas of need, the librarian will develop profiles. These will include the idiosyncracies of the more frequent clients. The user profiles will enrich the librarian's ability to select documents not only by topic, but also by all those attributes that contribute to "what it means to mean—how it suits my purposes."

The interface is nurtured and enlarged and elaborated. Few patrons would expect the new reference librarian to be as facile with and knowledgeable of individual representation schemes as a librarian who had been on the job for a year or more. So, too, we may imagine a digital system that gathers input from users and grows and becomes more elaborate in its representational capabilities.

Such an interface also assumes that at least some of the patrons will, upon occasion, be willing to take the time and effort to contribute to the system. The imagined community memory interface for the picture collection assumes only the most minimal representation of pictures at first. Patrons may have to do random searches. As a picture is found that is desirable, for whatever reason, a request box will appear on the computer screen asking if the patron would care to add subject headings or comments about the picture to the access system.

As more and more use is made of the system, many images will begin to accumulate descriptors. Some images, though, may accumulate few or none. This will reflect the needs of the community using the documents. The patron who might be served by an image with few or no community tags will still have the option to browse through the images not yet labeled. Figure 9.4 diagrams the basic interface.

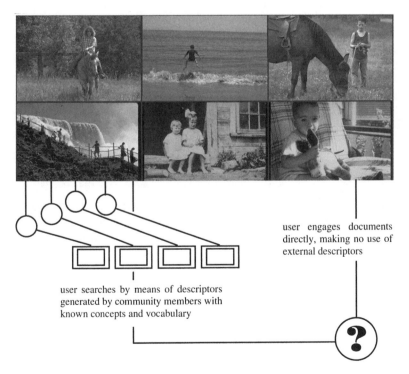

user engages documents directly, making no use of external descriptors

user searches by means of descriptors generated by community members with known concepts and vocabulary

Fig. 9.4. Community memory interface enables access by functional or adjectival descriptors applied by users with similar profiles.

Actually, because humans are so good at visual processing, browsing presents a powerful means of access to pictures. Research suggests that most people can distinguish a few images per second. Even at 2 images per second, one can examine over 100 images in a minute.

Implied in what has already been said about such a system is the acknowledgment that the bibliographic agency no longer holds the power or the burden of being the sole constructor of the representation system. The users acquire a significantly richer representation method, but must realize that it may take time for the digital system to become a fully developed partner.

It became apparent in casual conversations and small exercises in the classroom that the same people who thought it would be good and appropriate to have adjectival and functional access had a difficult time generating terms, phrases, or sentences to describe either their needs or the pictures. We suspect that this is the result of two factors: novelty and lack of general facility with image communication. Having users generate their own descriptors for any sort of document is not a common activity in most information systems. As suggested earlier, construction and description of images has no substantial history outside the art and commercial production realms. Pictures are not studied in most elementary schools to the degree that spoken and written language are studied. Although we live in a media-rich environment, critical and manipulative skills are still wanting.

Elicitation of Functional Descriptors

Elicitation of adjectival, functional descriptors is the first challenge in designing a community memory interface. One phase of research on access to digital images demonstrates a promising approach to descriptor elicitation. Fifteen images were transferred from 35mm slides to Kodak PhotoCD. Graduate students viewed the images on a high-resolution color monitor and filled out a one-page form for each of the pictures. A thumbnail version of each image was included in the packet of forms for reference. Each student was allowed 40 minutes to view and describe all 15 images.

Two goals were established at this point:

- To ease user construction of adjectival, functional descriptors

- To determine if the descriptors showed variation in both concept and depth

Easing user construction of descriptors depended on personal observation and casual conversations. A preliminary group of viewers was asked to "construct adjectival descriptors." They attempted, either on paper or verbally, to generate a phrase for each image in the mode of a Library of Congress Subject Heading. Several then commented that this was difficult. However, in subsequent conversation about individual pictures, the same people were able to tell little stories or imagine that they were describing this picture to someone else.

With this observation, we designed a form with three regions on the page:

- Caption

- Descriptive Words & Phrases

- Reactions

The word *caption* seems to have eliminated the perceived necessity to construct something formal. There were no complaints among three groups of 15 about the difficulty of construction. Captions were cute, clever, humorous, prosaic, directly tied to the objects in the image, and idiosyncratic. Table 9.1 demonstrates the variety of forms and concepts represented. (The images are shown in figure 9.5 on page 156.) This sample of captions presents a set of descriptors that are not topical in the sense of naming objects recorded in the images. Some use the images as metaphors for broader topics. Some imbue the images with an emotional component. Some present the interior monologue of a subject or presumed viewer. In each case, the descriptors go beyond topical description at the level of the document. They go to a higher or lower level of specificity or go beyond the nominal topicality altogether. In this sense, they all present the possibility of searches of a functional or nontopical sort.

Table 9.1
Sample Captions of Test Set of Images in figure 9.5.

What's Up, Doc?	You want me to what? Yeah, right!
Young man with a purpose	Boy, this is dumb!
Majestic waterfall	Nature's Power
Ride 'em cowcat	What have we got here?
A walk on the wild side	Home on the range
The one that got away	Helping a fallen friend
Door to the past	Where's the beef?
Painful lesson	Who? Me?
The American Way	End of summer
Off the deep end	Where'd I leave that bull?
Forever, I will live alone	Miles from nowhere
Where is the damned bull?	That's what friends are for!
Escape from unreality	Peekaboo
What is the future hiding?	The great outdoors
We told you to watch your step!	The dirt crop is doing well this year!
Playtime for Kitty	OK, Billy, you pull that way and I'll pull this way
Ouch!	I know I had a few beers, but how'd I get into this?
Didn't make it this time	Helping hands
Far from the Madding Crowd!	Lazy, hazy day
Up we go!	It's that tree, that big green one, right there!
Just a lazy day	One more ride

The segment labeled "Descriptive Words & Phrases" was used largely, though not exclusively, for prosaic listings of observed objects. These descriptors ranged from single words, to lists of single words, to sentences and paragraphs. Image attributes such as color, brightness, and composition were sometimes mentioned in this segment.

Personal responses, which it was felt would be especially adjectival, were elicited in the "Reactions" segment. Table 9.2 indicates that there were, indeed, personal reactions. The interesting challenge that still lies ahead is to collect enough data to determine if reactions cluster around a few concepts or whether they vary so widely as to be of little use to anyone but the originator of the description.

Table 9.2
Sample Descriptive Phrases Applied to Test Photographs in Figure 9.6

Horse, Pasture
Ocean horizon with small wave on beach; male kid playing
majestic tree; stables; white ranch fence
Elephant, close-up of eye; wrinkles
Trees, horse, rider, fence
Young, blond child next to sea; calm water, rocky beach
Cowboy with wrapped knee in a corral, looks upset, big belt buckle, ugly hat
Several cows on dry grassland with wire fence—cloudy day
Blue, sandy, rocky, blond boy
Cowboy, belt buckle, hat, pens, sadness
Lonely but beautiful
Door, wood, rock, mortar, old, hole in the door
Beautiful, powerful, dangerous
Home, barbed wire, steers, plains
Cat, plastic hobby horse, life
Gushy, cool, refreshing, soothing
Man against animal
Arid, warm
Cute, adorable cat
Uses for an old rocking horse
Little boat in the distance
Toy horse, yellow kitten, grass field
Child playing in ocean
Cowboy
Trailer on acreage
Children playing; neighborhood
Flag girl, rodeo, horses, Stars & Stripes
Cat in yard
Injured cowboy; walking cowboy
Trailer; farmland; plowed field
Woman on a horse holding the American flag at a rodeo
Waterfall
Cattle near a barbed-wire fence
Spring-like atmosphere
Nature and pretend nature at play
Peaceful ocean
Off-season for swimmers
Bandage on knee suggests tough ride
Belt Buckle still beams proudly
Fence does not fence a lot
Constructed crudely to keep cold out at all costs
School's out
Innocent-looking cat

Without quantitative measures or the testing of varying instruments, we cannot say that we have approached an optimal means of easing user input. However, the lack of complaints at the time of filling out the forms, or during questioning afterward, suggests that this instrument is, at least, adequate to the task.

The sample size is still too small to make significant generalizations about variety of concepts and variety of depth or level of specificity. Figure 9.6 on page 157, which presents the images and data for four of the pictures, demonstrates considerable variance. Indeed, some images elicited descriptors that are nearly opposites. For comparison purposes, figure 9.5 on page 156 presents subject headings in the manner of Library of Congress Subject Headings, applied to each of the test pictures by an art and architecture slide librarian.

Pictures are not words, but words can be used as representation tools, especially if those tools are put into the hands of the users. The rules for highlighting and the methods of coding are manifest to the users because they made them. Of course, this assumes either a certain homogeneity of users or availability of means for a patron to select search terms applied by users with some particular profile. Now, it may turn out that if there are enough users of the system, no matter how heterogenous they may be, several small clusters of very different types of description will develop for some pictures. Many patrons, then, would have available representations constructed by members of the microcommunity to which they belong.

Aboutness, in the functional sense we have used, is a powerful representation because it directly includes the user's knowledge state in the representation process. Evidence so far suggests that a community memory interface is one method of integrating aboutness into the retrieval process. It may just take some time to engineer the dynamic learning system required for the implementation of requests based on aboutness.

Notes

1.   M. E. Maron, "On Indexing, Retrieval, and the Meaning of About," *Journal of the American Society for Information Science* 28 no. 1 (1977): 38-43. For other foundational thoughts on the meaning of *about* in information retrieval, see S. E. Robertson, "Between Aboutness and Meaning," in *The Analysis of Meaning: Informatics* 5, edited by MacCafferty and Gray (London: Aslib, 1979); and Patrick Wilson, *Two Kinds of Power: An Essay on Bibliographical Control* (Berkeley: University of California Press, 1968).

2.   David Novitz, *Pictures and Their Use in Communication* (The Hague: Nijhoff, 1977).

3.   Martin Fischler and Oscar Firschein, *Intelligence: The Eye, the Brain and the Computer* (Reading, Mass.: Addison-Wesley, 1987).

4.   Brian O'Connor, "Access to Moving Image Documents: Background Concepts and Proposals for Surrogates for Moving Image Documents," *Journal of Documentation* 41, no. 4 (1985): 209-20.

Lakes—Shorelines
Outdoor Recreation
  for Children

Ocean
Boys
Portraits

Lakes—Shorelines
Trees in Winter

Lakes—Shorelines
Environment and
  Children

Cats
Toy Horses
Merry-Go-Round
Art

Cowboys
Horsemen and
Horsewomen

Mountains—Idaho
Ranch Houses
Trailers

Building, Brick
Commercial Building
Shop Fronts

Building, Stone
Building, Brick
Blinds

Roller Skating
Outdoor Recreation
  for Children

Cowboys
Rodeos
Horse Sports

Niagara Falls
Wild and Scenic Rivers

Fig. 9.5. Standard subject headings for pictures used in the text file.

humorous	curiosity	cute
nice	cute	relaxing
enchantment	cute	cute
cute	tender	warmth
soft & lovable	sweet	cute
surprise	delight	joy
natural		

all responses—not everyone responded

tension	anticipation	anxiety
ruggedness	anger	disgust
determination	courage	rural scene
work clothes	calloused	tough & rugged
unfeeling	tough	resolute
determined	another era	Kansas
needs a bath	discouraging	strong
face a challange	disappointment	

dusty & dry	solitary	isolated
peaceful	isolated	lonely
peace	ownership	pride
independence	desolate	lovely
relaxing	boring	barren & sad
vast	desolate	peaceful
Colorado	Arizona	beautiful
Indian reservation		

expansiveness	quiet	peaceful
free of burdens	view from porch	rural road
bucolic	desolate	rugged
prairie life	simple life	serene
memories	Texas	hot & dusty
dry	thirsty	tired
Texas	prisoners	suffering
cold pasture	winter morning	heat
summer	dryness	never ending

Fig. 9.6. Variance in "Reaction" responses to test images.

Chapter 10
Creek Pebbles, Chaos, Vertov, and Dynagraphics

Creek pebbles in a bag are one metaphor proposed by William Least Heat-Moon for organizing thoughts about a journey one has just made. Standing on a hill in rural Kansas, he asks if one should just take one's impressions, insights, and facts and let them fall as they will, like pebbles scooped up from a creek and tossed into a bag, taking on their own order. The random order may not be entirely satisfactory, but it can be instructive. We want to come to know the pebbles and their environment and their workings individually and collectively. The subtitle of the book resulting from Heat-Moon's travels and contemplations, *A Deep Map*, offers a provocative concept for our considerations of reducing search space.[1]

Our explorations in indexing and abstracting have had us venture over a large and varied terrain. Some regions have been criss-crossed several times; others have been sighted only in the distance. We strongly suggest the study of works on travel and exploration because indexing, abstracting, and classifying bear more than a metaphorical relationship to the mapping of geographical territory. The concepts of how one comes to know things about an area hold whether we speak of an intellectual or geographical area. Indeed, it may be only a matter of convenience to make the distinction at all. We might also say that it is critical that we come to know the knowledge territories of those for whom we construct information systems, or at least how to account for their ways of knowing.

Explorations seldom simply end. They yield interesting insights, with luck, and perhaps material of immediate utility. They also stimulate reflection upon where we have been, where we would now like to go, whither we would like to return, and how we are to make sense of it all.

Reflections

It is time to look back briefly on where we have been and then to scoop up some more pebbles to help us think of where we might next travel. We set out with a few pathways chosen and some explicitly ignored. This was not to be a survey of indexing and abstracting practices, nor was it to be a manual for any particular sort of indexing and abstracting practice. The maps for those areas have been well constructed and are sufficiently numerous.

We followed some paths through ideas on representation and how one thing stands for another. The problems that can arise when representation of questions and documents is not thought out were examined through exercises and thought experiments. Possible responses to the problems of such representation were considered.

The seeming contradiction of increasing access by reducing a priori conceptual tagging was explored in some depth. This would be accomplished by representing only the physically present text, pointing out major discontinuities (hills and valleys) on the document's landscape, and enabling the patron to make concept and value judgments. The ability of a digital environment to process large amounts of physical data was the foundation of such an approach to mapping documents to reduce search time.

The seemingly opposite approach of using the machine to gather conceptual judgments and make them useable was also examined. Here the user group would help to train the system and thus craft it to the idiosyncrasies of the user group.

In most of our considerations and exercises, we examined different means of changing the locus of representation, so as to include the user to some greater degree. This suggested possible changes in the nature of the relationship of some users to some systems. In many ways, those changes mirror the relation one might expect to have with the neighborhood bookstore owner or video dealer or the good reference librarian. That is, one develops a relationship through which the idiosyncrasies of interests and seeking habits become known and can be incorporated into the system. Indeed, the system (in the form of the neighborhood bookseller) might be able to predict that a work would be of interest even before you came looking.

The possible search space is increasing by leaps and bounds; search time is not. The challenge is to design systems for reducing search time in a useful manner. The variety in question types and searching styles adds to the challenge. We might suggest at this point a guiding principle: *There should be no surprises for the patron.* That is, when a patron makes use of an access tool, the document to which that tool leads ought not to disappoint the patron ("That's not what I thought it would be about").

Pebbles

Here we will pick up more pebbles. They are scooped up with no particular plan. However, they do come from the same creek bed. They should illuminate, substantiate, challenge, and expand our thoughts on where we have been and where we ought to go.

Representing knowledge might almost be a description of what we have been considering. It is, in fact, the general term for the problems of encoding massive amounts of data and establishing procedures for embedding reasoning stratagems within computers. What can we learn from such studies that could be used to undergird our concerns for user-centric access?

Genetic algorithms are based on Darwinian evolution principles; in essence, they can be used to cause elements more suited to an environment to become more and more prevalent. As with breeding animals, one starts with a population that exhibits, to some degree, the desired population. In successive generations, one breeds the offspring showing the greatest degree of the desired characteristic. Eventually, one has a group that displays the characteristic to a high degree. What ways can we think of to "breed" question and document attributes? Can we make significant use of Blair's suggestions for using genetic algorithms to produce the most useful subject descriptors from a seed group of descriptors?

The *physically present* was the subject of some of our explorations. What might we ask about the physically present document collection? What aspects of browsing paper stacks warrant inclusion in electronic environments? Are the cues present in book collections—color, size, physical location—sufficiently important to include (in some analog form) in electronic environments? Does the social interaction with a physically present intermediary differ in important ways from searching by oneself?

Complexity is sometimes defined as the narrow zone between stasis and chaos. It is a zone where small changes can sometimes yield major changes. Does this have any significant relationship to creative activity? Does the creative person purposely put aside stasis, generate changes, and hope for a significant result? Is this like browsing, and, if so, can we use the mathematics underlying complexity to aid in the browsing process?

The *nature of knowledge* would seem to be an area warranting considerable attention from those concerned with providing linkages between the knowledge state of a patron and the knowledge state represented by a document. The field becomes more compelling as one sees philosophers, engineers, mathematicians, and biologists examining similar questions within similar frameworks. Plotkin suggests that "knowledge . . . is a way of incorporating the thing known into the knower."[2] Even within the individual, he argues, this is a process that resembles the genetic algorithm and the engineer's "generate, test, regenerate."[3] What is there that we might incorporate into the very way we conceive of access to documents within such thinking? If documents and questions are both representations of knowledge states, can we treat them as the same sort of entity to any value? Might it even be possible to regenerate questions in an informed manner?

The *Internet* was once a means for a relatively small number of researchers to share data and concepts; today, it is common fare in newspaper articles and television news coverage. With millions of people around the world not only attached but, in many instances, also generating new material, what is to be done in terms of access systems? Can it really be a good idea to apply systems of classification resembling those from print libraries to the Internet? Do we really need any sort of access systems beyond those that are developed ad hoc? Many Internet users speak of the delight they take in the lack of authoritative control in any aspect of the system. When information is needed, a request can be made to a subset of the Internet community. Could this be more user-centric than standard access systems?

Browsing has long been seen as a significant search method. Much effort has been invested in Internet browsers. Are these really browsers or are they grazers? What are the on-line analogs to moving about in the stacks? Could knowbots act as surrogate browsers? Biologists and biomathematicians are studying the food-searching strategies of various animals. What in these studies might augment the operations research approach introduced by Morse?

Classification, suggests Estes, "is basic to all of our intellectual activities."[4] Yet, despite tremendous strides in our understanding and 2,000 years of written examination of the issues, "we are usually in the dark about the basis for human cognitive performance." We do have some evidence, though, to suggest that multiple categories are held for the same entity. We have moved away from the strictly Aristotelian concept of classification to various systems with taxonomies of classifications based on varying degrees of membership. How do fuzzy sets and probabilistic classification speak to the design of access systems?

Electronic journals have begun to make significant contributions to academia. Does the possibility of linked responses from readers offer a means of ad hoc review that might enrich the access environment? As many issues are discussed in listservs and newsgroups on the Internet, ought we to think of providing access to these discussions? Does keyword access provide a sufficient mechanism?

Chaos has become an almost fashionable topic even in the popular press. Few of these reports operate in the realm of chaos as, in Kellert's terms, "the qualitative study of unstable aperiodic behavior in deterministic nonlinear dynamical systems."[5] Such definitions are sometimes inappropriately used to bolster nondeterministic approaches to social systems. Yet we might ask if there is some aspect of chaos studies could be applied to question-asking and document-seeking practices. Does the study of chaos and the attendant complexity lead to deeper understandings of epistemology? Does this line of thought lead to deeper foundations in our understanding of the very nature of information?

Vertov is one of the great names in the history of filmmaking; an early Soviet film artist whose personal vision and lucid insights into the nature of film communication still bear close consideration. However, he is not exactly a household name and his work is difficult to find in local video stores. A film database accessible over the Internet provides cogent and detailed profiles of film artists such as Vertov, so that one can read of his life and artistic philosophy even if the library is closed. One can also find the Siskel and Ebert "Ten Best" lists of films from 1979 through 1991 (as of this writing). This provides interesting reading and speaks to the discussion in chapter 9 about film reviewers and aboutness decisions.

Infobits, a service of the Institute for Academic Technology, acts as a surrogate monitor for people in the education field, sifting through numerous listserv publications and other electronic fora to find material of value to the clientele. One item in a 1995 issue is instructive. An article in *Scientific American* is cited, along with an abstract highlighting the aspects of interest to educators and subscription information. Also included is a World Wide Web address for an electronic archive mentioned in the abstract. Thus, we have a tailored abstract and helpful logistic information presented in a customized fashion (if not individualized). Search space and the costs of monitoring the information environment have been reduced for the individual user.

The flood of information on the Internet is the topic of the abstracted article in *Infobits.* The author, Stix, notes that although there are concerns about the volume of traffic, paper journals in the scholarly disciplines are not without serious problems, not the least of which are cost and timeliness.[6] Even good access to material no longer useful because of age does not constitute a good system.

There is probably some danger in speaking too closely of details of today's information environment. Surely much of this will be archaic within weeks. Yet, we should not lose sight of the fact that the quantitative changes in data availability are leading qualitative changes in the sorts of questions that can be asked and the arrangements within which they can be asked. It may be of use to look to the past. Classicist Arrowsmith suggests that *changes in media* will not, in and of themselves, generate better conditions; we must continue to grapple with what it means to be fully human.[7] This may mean, among other things, careful consideration of what sorts of questions can be asked. Information exists within societal constructs. Destruction of the Alexandrian Library, the persecution of women as witches, and censorship disputes in schools are but a few of the most obvious examples of the dangers inherent in the social construction of knowledge.

Bounty hunters[8] traverse search space and have devised methods of reducing, synthesizing, and analyzing data. They spend most of their time initiating simultaneous search subroutines and monitoring the value of each routine. They also come to understand the environment and thought patterns of those for whom they are searching. They make substantial use of small but significant pieces of information. How do they know where to look for these small bits of information and what to make of them? What might we learn from bounty hunters to enhance the abilities of search intermediaries?

Artists must constantly struggle with the manner in which to present their views of the object/event space. What is the proper mix of novelty and familiarity? What can we learn from artists about repackaging information to make it most useful to individual clients? What are the means artists use to make new connections and new combinations? How might we incorporate this sort of knowledge into the design of access systems?

Who are the other people whose professional insights into humanity and use of information could contribute to our understanding of information and its use? *What* must we know, so that when a patron walks in the door or logs onto a computer system, or uses whatever mediating systems may become available, we can provide the most powerful, the most highly crafted, the most precise tools available to help that person meet with success?

In the midst of gathering these pebbles, an interesting little piece came across the Internet. It is quoted at length here because it speaks to our reflections on our explorations.

> [B]ut I wonder if we are in a bibliographic world. It doesn't take much to see a future where the NET itself is the most important information utility in the world for the simple reason that it includes the author— which libraries could never include . . . along with a tremendous amount of non-textual, essentially non-bibliographic stuff, multimedia in nature, associative in personal human terms. Libraries will be part of this smorgasbord, . . . probably a background database which supports billions of Web pages which are not developed at, by, or for cataloging departments. The prototype of this world already exists and will only grow. Most of us search this mess every day. It's a mess to us because we are bibliographic people, but the world we knew seems to have become *dynagraphic*. . . . There is an interesting new intro [to the reissue of McLuhan's *Understanding Media*] by Lewis Lapham. He lists a range of what he calls McLuhan's Homeric epithets . . . one of which is a contrast between print/classification and electromedia pattern recognition. Bibliographic is essentially static, dead information—print is very hard

to change quickly—which can be pondered, considered, and classified. Dynagraphic information . . . is . . . . well, dynamic, moves faster than a speeding URL . . . . Add into this pot world-wide access with potentially all of the world's languages and conceptual categories and what sort of training, education, skills do you plan for?

—Thom[9]

There are still too many documents. During the time from the writing of the first chapter of this book and doing the final editing, the number of documents available has increased. Web sites have multiplied, books and magazines have not disappeared, and new hybrid media have been developed. People are now beginning to wonder how to organize just the bookmarks they accumulate for interesting World Wide Web sites. National Public Radio is but one of the audio sites on the Web. Digital Video Disc promises extraordinarily high-quality audio and video. Recording CD-ROM units are now priced at consumer levels.

Humans long ago invented means for storing information outside individual brains. This invention of recorded information offers data and insights no longer bound to a single time and place. We need no longer depend on personal experience or the recollections of those with whom we have physical contact. Yet, the search space presented by the mass of recorded documents present us with a significant dilemma—how are we to choose and use the "right documents"?

This chapter has been a reflection on where we have been and where we might want to go in our explorations. We have tried to generate questions that will challenge us and enlighten our efforts at reducing search time for people in need of information. We have scooped up a few more pebbles to expand our thoughts. We have, perhaps, gotten a feel for the territory and for the various paths within it. Certainly there will be frustrations that we did not discover a simple mechanism, a single prescription, a main highway across the territory. Yet this can also be the source of wonder and encouragement.

Notes ————————————————————————

1. William Least Heat-Moon, *PrairyErth (a deep map)* (Boston: Houghton Mifflin, 1991). Note that the Library of Congress Cataloging-in-Publication data lists these subject headings for the work: Chase County (Kan.)—Description and Travel; Chase County (Kan.)—History, Local; and Heat-Moon, William Least—Journeys—Kansas—Chase County. Though one cannot deny that the work is set within Chase County, the implications of the work are far greater than a mere descriptive travelog. To the degree that it is the "modern day Walden" (review by Richard West in the *Chicago Sun-Times*), or the "*Moby Dick* of American history" (Bill McKibben in *The Hungry Mind Review*, or a "recapturing . . . of the American grain (Paul Theroux in *The New York Times Book Review*), the first two subject headings seem too local to be of use to readers not familiar with Kansas or the author. It is difficult to imagine such a reader thinking, "I would like a work on the manner in which the ordinary and local can inform our understanding of the larger enterprise—I think I will look under, let's see, ah! Chase County, Kansas." Though, of course, if one is in Chase County and seeking a good guide book, *PrairyErth* can fill that requirement also.

2. Henry Plotkin, *Darwin Machines and the Nature of Knowledge* (Cambridge, Mass.: Harvard University Press, 1994), 13.

3. See, for example, Fred Hapgood, *Up the Infinite Corridor: MIT and the Technological Imagination* (Reading, Mass.: Addison-Wesley, 1993).

4. William K. Estes, *Classification and Cognition* (New York: Oxford University Press, 1994), 4.

5. Stephen H. Kellert, *In the Wake of Chaos: Unpredictable Order in Dynamical Systems* (Chicago: University of Chicago Press, 1993), 2.

6. Gary Stix, "The Speed of Write," *Scientific American* 271, no. 6 (December 1994): 106-11.

7. W. Arrowsmith, "Film as Educator," *Journal of Aesthetic Education* 3, no. 3 (1969): 75-83; David Bianculli, *Teleliteracy: Taking Television Seriously* (New York: Continuum, 1992) 75-83.

8. Bounty hunting is an information profession, according to David C. O'Connor, a successful private investigator working with the judicial system. He notes a similarity to scholarly searching in the frequent paucity of clues, the constant monitoring of several lines of inquiry, and the potential importance of the slightest glimpse. Both scholarly searching and criminal investigation resemble sailing: Sometimes the winds are at one's back and progress is steady; at other times one must maneuver as best one can, hoping for general forward progress.

9. Personal communication with Thom Gillespie (via e-mail), 1995.

Appendix

```
REM $STATIC
SUB opener
REM *** Extracts Key Words ***
SHARED cow, bull, ox, xlnt, kao
bull = 0
SHARED compar$, checker$, titl$
CLS
INPUT "Name of file "; titl$
BEEP

FOR who = 1 TO 15000: NEXT who
xlnt = TIMER
OPEN titl$ + ".txt" FOR INPUT AS #1
WHILE NOT EOF(1)
compar$ = INPUT$(1, 1)
LET bull = bull + 1


IF 64  ASC(compar$) AND ASC(compar$)  123 AND ASC(compar$)
   91 AND ASC(compar$)  93 THEN checker$ = checker$ + compar$
IF compar$ = " " OR compar$ = "." THEN CALL purple: kao = kao + 1

WEND
CLOSE #1
CLS
BEEP
LOCATE 20, 20
PRINT "EXTRACTION COMPLETE"
END SUB
```

Fig. A.1. QBASIC code for simple word-extraction routine.

```
SUB purple
SHARED checker$, ox, bull, titl$, xlnt, kao

REM *** checks stop list
gut$ = LEFT$(titl$, 6)
OPEN gut$ + "wo" FOR APPEND AS #2
OPEN gut$ + "nu" FOR APPEND AS #3
IF checker$  "" THEN
    RESTORE
    FOR a = 1 TO 509
        READ s$
        IF checker$ = s$ THEN
            checker$ = "": CLOSE #2: CLOSE #3
            EXIT SUB
        END IF
    NEXT a

LOCATE 20, 15
PRINT checker$, kao, TIMER - xlnt
WRITE #2, checker$
z = ((bull + 1) - (LEN(checker$)))
WRITE #3, z
checker$ = ""
ox = ox + 1
END IF
CLOSE #2
CLOSE #3

CLS


END SUB
```

Fig. A.2. Routine for checking words against stop list.

Additional Readings

American National Standards Institute, *American National Standard for Library and Information Sciences and Related Publishing Practices—Basic Criteria for Indexes,* (New York: ANSI, 1984). Read this together with later articles on updating of the Z39.4 standards, for example: J. D. Anderson, "Standards for Indexing: Revising the American National Standard Guidelines Z39.4." *Journal of the American Society for Information Science* 45, no. 8 (1994): 628-36.

Bates, Marcia. "The Design of Browsing and Berrypicking Techniques for the On-line Search Interface." *Online Review* 13, no. 5 (1989): 407–24.

————. "Subject Access in Online Catalogs: A Design Model." *Journal of the American Society for Information Science* 37, no. 6 (1986): 357–76.

Belkin, Nicholas. "Anomalous States of Knowledge as a Basis for Information Retrieval." *Canadian Journal of Information Science* 5 (1980): 434–43.

Bell, W. J. *Searching Behavior: The Behavioral Ecology of Finding Resources.* (New York: Chapman and Hall, 1991).

Blair, David C., and M. E. Maron. "Full-Text Information Retrieval: Further Analysis and Clarification." *Information Processing & Management* 26, no. 3 (1990): 437–47.

Boyce, Bert. "Beyond Topicality: A Two Stage View of Relevance and the Retrieval Process." *Information Processing & Management* 18, no. 3 (1982): 105–09.

Brajnik, Giorgio, Giovanni Guida, and Carlo Tasso. "User Modeling in Intelligent Information Retrieval." *Information Processing & Management* 23, no. 4 (1987): 305–20.

Buckland, Michael. "On Types of Search and the Allocation of Library Resources." *Journal of the American Society for Information Science* 30, no. 3 (1979): 143–47.

169

Buckland, Michael, and Frederic Gray. "The Relationship Between Recall and Precision." *Journal of the American Society for Information Science* 45, no. 1 (1994): 12–19.

Buckland, Michael, Barbara Norgard, and Christian Plaunt. "Filing, Filtering, and the First Few Found." *Information Technology and Libraries* 12, no. 3 (1993): 311–20.

Cari, Lucretius. *De Rerum Natura* (Madison: University of Wisconsin Press, 1968). Edited with introduction and commentary by W. E. Smith and S. B. Smith.

Cassi, P. Mussio, M. Padula, M. Protti, and G. Tonolli. "Relational Tools to Manage Pictorial Information." *Journal of Information Science* 18 (1992): 375–98.

Chu, Clara, and Ann O'Brien. "Subject Analysis: The Critical First Stage in Indexing."*Journal of Information Science* 19 (1993): 439–54.

Cleveland, Donald, and Ana Cleveland. *Introduction to Indexing and Abstracting* (Englewood, Colo.: Libraries Unlimited, 1990).

Cooper, William S. "Getting Beyond Boole." *Information Processing & Management* 24, no. 3 (1988): 243–48.

Damashek, Marc. "Gauging Similarity with n-Grams: Language-Independent Categorization of Text." *Science* 267 (Feb. 1995): 843–48.

De May, Marc. *The Cognitive Paradigm* (Boston: D. Reidel, 1982).

Eco, Umberto. *The Name of the Rose* (San Diego: Warner, 1983). Translated from Italian by William Weaver.

Ellis, David. "The Physical and Cognitive Paradigms in Information Retrieval Research." *Journal of Documentation* 48, no. 1 (1992): 45–64.

Froehlich, Thomas J. "Relevance Reconsidered—Towards an Agenda for the 21st Century: Introduction to Special Issue on Relevance Research." *Journal of the American Society for Information Science* 45, no. 3 (1994): 124–34.

Gardner, Howard. *The Mind's New Science: A History of the Cognitive Revolution* (New York: Basic Books, 1987).

Ide, Nancy. "A Statistical Measure of Theme and Structure." *Computers and the Humanities* 23 (1989): 277-83.

Jones, Karen Sparck, and J. I. Tait. "Automatic Search Term Variant Generation." *Journal of Documentation* 40, no. 1 (1984): 50–66.

Lancaster, F. W. *Indexing and Abstracting in Theory and Practice* (Champaign: University of Illinois, 1991).

Larson, Ray R. "Evaluation of Advanced Retrieval Techniques in an Experimental Online Catalog." *Journal of the American Society for Information Science* 43, no. 1 (1992): 34–53.

———. "Experiments in Automatic Library of Congress Classification." *Journal of the American Society for Information Science* 43, no. 2 (1992): 130–48.

Library Trends 38, no. 4 (1990). Special Issue on "Intellectual Access to Graphic Information."

Macbeth, Doug. "Classroom Encounters with the Unspeakable: 'Do You See, Danell?' " Presented to the Annual Conference of the American Anthropological Association, 1991.

————. "Glances, Trances, and Their Relevance for a Visual Sociology." This paper was first presented to the 4th Annual Conference on Liberal Arts and the Education of Artists, 1990.

Metz, Christian. *Film Language: A Semiotics of Cinema* (New York: Oxford University Press, 1974).

Mostafa, Javed. "Digital Image Representation and Access." *Annual Review of Information Science and Technology (ARIST)* 29 (1994): 91–135.

Mulvaney, Nancy C. *Indexing Books* (Chicago: University of Chicago Press, 1994).

Olaisen, Johan. "Toward a Theory of Information Seeking Behavior Among Scientists and Scholars." Ph.D. diss., University of California, Berkeley, 1984.

Petry, Frederick, Bill Buckles, Devaraya Prabhu, and Donald Kraft. "Fuzzy Information Retrieval Using Genetic Algorithms and Relevance Feedback." *Proceedings of the 56th Annual Meeting of the American Society for Information Science* (1993).

Rietman, Edward. *Genesis Redux: Experiments Creating Artificial Life* (New York: Windcrest/McGraw-Hill, 1994).

Rosch, Eleanor. "Principles of Categorization." In *Cognition and Categorization.* Edited by E. Rosch and B. Lloyd (Potomac, Md.: Erlbaum, 1977).

Sagan, Carl, and Ann Druyan. *Shadows of Forgotten Ancestors: A Search for Who We Are* (New York: Random House, 1992).

Salton, Gerald. "Developments in Automatic Text Retrieval." *Science* 253 (1991): 974.

Salton, Gerald, J. Annan, C. Buckley, and A. Singhal. "Automatic Analysis, Theme Generation, and Summarization of Machine-Readable Texts." *Science* 264 (1994): 1421.

Schmidt, Klaus M. "Can There Be a Symbiosis Between Natural Language Meaning and Concept? Conceptual Analysis in the Humanities." *Proceedings of the 48th Annual Meeting of the American Society for Information Science* (1985): 358.

Stone, Alva T. "That Elusive Concept of 'Aboutness': The Year's Work in Subject Analysis, 1992." *Library Research and Technical Services* 37, no. 3 (1993): 277–98.

Thagard, Paul. *Conceptual Revolutions* (Princeton, N.J.: Princeton University Press, 1992).

Thompson, Paul. "A Combination of Expert Opinion Approach to Probabilistic Information Retrieval, Part 1: The Conceptual Model; and Part 2: Mathematical Model of CEO Model 3." *Information Processing & Management* 26, no. 3 (1990): 371–94.

van Rijsbergen, Dunlop, and C. J. van Rijsbergen. "Hypermedia and Free Text Retrieval." *Information Processing & Management* 29, no. 3 (1993): 287–98.

Waltz, David L. "Memory-based Reasoning." *Natural and Artificial Parallel Computation.* Edited by M. A. Arbib and J. A. Robinson (Cambridge, Mass.: MIT Press, 1990): 251–76.

Wang, Peiling, and Dagobert Soergel. "Beyond Topical Relevance: Document Selection Behavior of Real Users of IR Systems." *Proceedings of the 56th Annual Meeting of the American Society for Information Science* 30 (1993).

Weber, Karen, and Alex Poon. "Marquee: A Tool for Real-Time Video Logging." Xerox Palo Alto Research Center research paper developed for submission to the 1994 Association for Computing Machinery Conference on Human Factors in Computing Systems Conference.

Weinberg, Bella Hass. "Why Indexing Fails the Researcher." *The Indexer* 16, no. 1 (April, 1988): 3–6.

Wilson, Patrick. "Situational Relevance." *Information Storage and Retrieval* 9 (1973): 457–71.

Winston, Patrick Henry, and Sarah Alexandra Shellard, eds. *Artificial Intelligence at MIT: Expanding Frontiers* (Cambridge, Mass.: MIT Press, 1990).

Woo, Janice. "Indexing: At Play in the Fields of Postmodernism." *Visual Resources* 10 (1994): 283–93.

———. "The Relationship Between What We Know and How We Classify: Some Philosophical Bases for Inquiry." *Proceedings of the 5th ASIS SIG/CR Classification Research Workshop* (1994): 197-210.

Index

There is a certain irony to putting together a static paper index to a work on dynamic and user-centered access. We are at a transitional phase in the construction and use of documents. We are bound to experience many instances of irony at such a time.

No surprises was the guiding phrase during the compilation of this map to the book's contents. Trying to accommodate publisher guidelines is important so that users have a familiar-looking tool, as well as to meet production constraints. Yet, there may also be reason to violate consistency for utility.

When an indexer has only one level and one size of index with which to work, the balance between sufficient depth and detail on the one hand and annoying clutter on the other is a major problem. A few points about the process of indexing this book may be of some benefit to the reader in understanding where and how the balance was struck in this instance.

The entire book was put through a word-extraction program similar to that explained in the text, stripping stop list words, yet leaving a list of many thousands in place. These remaining words were alphabetized and their addresses within the book sorted. Each and every word was examined with an eye to its likely utility in the index. The assumption was made that some people would skim the index as a means of evaluating the book, but that the majority of users would be readers wanting to access information.

Some words, such as *book*, *document*, *collection*, *patrons*, *research*, *system*, and *word* appear with such frequency that they are of little value in guidance. Some index entries do not list every instance of the listed word. Some significant words are also used in examples or in less-than-significant ways in some parts of the text. For example, *topic* is used at times to mean a substantive conceptual aspect of a document, and at other times in the phrase "the topic of the article is. . . ."

The terms chosen, it is hoped, will provide sufficient detail to allow readers the access they need to the text.